VISIT THE CITY

D
Mak

DRESDEN AT A GLANCE

- The Historic City
- The Frauenkirche
- The Neustadt
- Strolling and Shopping
- Schloss Pillnitz
- Loschwitz
- The Zwinger

3 Days in

Content

Welcome to Dresden	4
About Dresden	6

Day 1 · In the baroque residence

The Historic City – On Europe's balcony (⌛2 h)	10
The Frauenkirche and Green Vault – Treasures (⌛2 h)	16

Day 2 · Strolling & Shopping

The Neustadt – Baroque and the Colorful Republic (⌛3 h)	22
Strolling and Shopping – Around Altmarkt and Prager Strasse (⌛3 h)	26

Day 3 · Along the big river

Schloss Pillnitz – Summerresidence (⌛2 h)	30
Loschwitz – The Blue Wonder (⌛2 h)	32
The Zwinger – Old Masters and celestial globes (⌛2 h)	34

Service

Hotels	38
Cafés and Lunch	42
Restaurants	44
Pubs and Beer Gardens	46
Bars and Nightlife	48
Wellness	50
Culture	52
Museums	56
Shopping	58
Useful Adresses	60
Dresden´s History	62
Register	64

Legende

- ⌛ Length of walk
- ◆ Opening times/ departure times
- ▲ Transport stop
- ➤ See page

Welcome

© BKB Verlagsgesellschaft mbH
All rights reserved
3/8/16

Editor in chief:
Dr. Brigitte Hintzen-Bohlen

Design:
Andreas Ossig
BKB Verlagsgesellschaft mbH

Translation:
John Sykes

Printed by:
Brandt GmbH, Bonn

ISBN 978-3-940914-71-2

All entries and information in this guide have been conscientiously researched and carefully checked. However, it is not always possible to rule out errors completely. We are therefore happy to receive suggestions for corrections and improvements.

BKB Verlagsgesellschaft mbH
Auerstraße 4
50733 Köln
Telephone +49 (0)221/9521460
Telefax   +49 (0)221/5626446
www.bkb-verlag.de
mail@bkb-verlag.de

... the capital of Saxony, with its with its unique buildings and the impressive man-made landscape of the Elbe valley, world-famous collections of art and legendary reputation as a city of music, not to mention the unique landscape of the Elbe valley.

Augustus the Strong and his son Frederick Augustus II were the rulers who created the city celebrated by poets as "Florence on the Elbe". They collected treasures from all over the world and brought innumerable artists to their court. Carl Maria Weber, Richard Wagner, Gottfried Semper and the artists of "Die Brücke" are just some of those who made Dresden's reputation as a city of art and culture.

to Dresden …

In the space of only a few hours, in February 1945, the city was reduced to smouldering rubble. Today, thanks to the determination of the people of Dresden to rebuild, we can once again admire the unique silhouette on the Elbe which inspired Canaletto's paintings 200 years ago. In 1945 the restoration of the Baroque Zwinger started; today, following the rebuilding of the Frauenkirche, the Dresden panorama of old is complete.

There is much more for visitors to discover in the Saxon capital, from the unconventional young scene in the New Town and the idyllic wine-growing village of Loschwitz to the palace of culture, synagogue and Transparent Factory: Dresden has its own blend of traditional and modern style. Today the city is an economic powerhouse, a centre of high-tech industry with an exemplary scientific infrastructure.

In addition to the culture, Dresden is a great place for enjoying life. In all parts of the city, pubs and restaurants serve food from around the world. Locals and visitors flock to the beer gardens in the meadows on the river, where paddle steamers pass by on excursions up and down the Elbe. For all those who come here for a lifestyle with a southern European touch, it is easy to understand what makes the "Florence of the north" so attractive.

About Dresden

● SILICON SAXONY is the name given to the region around Dresden in reference to Silicon Valley in California, the world's best-known area for the semi-conductor and computer industry, because most companies here work in the fields of microelectronics, information and biotechnology and electronics, and because the city is a leading European centre of semi-conductor manufacture.

● With the Technical University of Dresden, the University for Technology and Business, many establishments of the Fraunhofer Institute, Max Planck Institute and Leibniz Gemeinschaft, as well as the networks and centres of excellence that have emerged from them, Dresden has the HIGHEST CONCENTRATION OF RESEARCH AND DEVELOPMENT in the technical and scientific field in the former East Germany.

● Right up to the 20th century, the Mathematical-Physical Salon was the Greenwich of Saxony, as the OFFICIAL TIME for Dresden and Saxony was established in the observatory of the Physical Cabinet in the Zwinger.

● At an international conference on problems of computer technology, the German term INFORMATIK was specified as the equivalent to the English expression "computer science" and the French "informatique" on 25 February 1968 in Dresden.

● 8,425 old stones have been reused in the FRAUENKIRCHE – 45 per cent of the historic fabric of the church.

- The oak tree called the SÄNGER-EICHE (singers' oak) was planted in the meadow at the foot of the Waldschlösschen Bridge in 1865 on the occasion of the first Deutsches Sängerbundesfest (Festival of the German Choral Society).

- In Radebeul near Dresden the author KARL MAY created the stories and characters of his Wild West novels, which have delighted generations of children and young people to this day.

- Following the founding of Germany's first cigarette factory in Dresden in 1862, this company launched the world's FIRST FILTER CIGARETTE in 1936. It was advertised as having "mild, clean smoke" that "preserves good health".

- The BEER MAT also comes from Dresden: in 1892 Robert Sputh from Dresden patented his process for making so-called poured-fibre mats with a diameter of 107 millimetres and a thickness of 5 millimetres. He poured a paper mash into moulds and left them to dry overnight. His dimensions remain the standard to this day!

- By baking a Dresden Stollen cake weighing 2,720 kilograms for the first Stollenfest in 1994, the bakers and pastry cooks of Dresden found their way into the GUINNESS BOOK OF RECORDS, and improved on their own record several times in the following years.

- The Christmas-season sweet known as a DOMINOSTEIN (domino piece) was invented in 1934 by Herbert Wendler from Dresden.

- With events on 60 days, the FILM NIGHTS BY THE ELBE are Germany's longest open-air film festival.

- With 15 students' clubs, Dresden is the leading centre for STUDENTS' CLUBS, run by students for students.

3 Days in

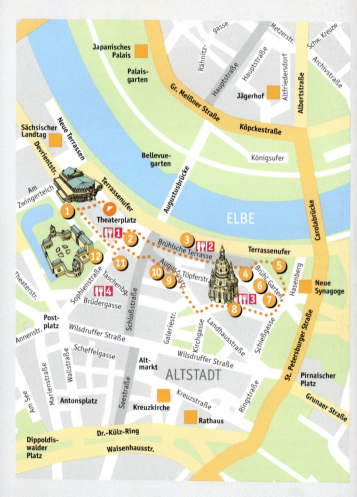

1. Semper Opera House
2. St. Trinitas Cathedral
3. Brühl Terrace
4. Academy of Arts
5. Brühlscher Garten
6. Fortifications
7. Albertinum
8. Frauenkirche
9. Stallhof
10. Royal Palace
11. Green Vault/Armoury
12. Zwinger

🍴1 Italienisches Dörfchen
🍴2 Café Vis-a-Vis
🍴3 Grand Cafés & Restaurants
🍴4 Classic American Bar

Day 1

The Historic City

The Historic City (⏱2h) 10
The Frauenkirche and Green Vault (⏱2h) 16

3 Days in

from 1 pm

On Europe's balcony
The Historic City Centre

A walk through the historic city centre takes you to an ensemble of buildings from the Baroque and Renaissance periods and the 19th century that are unique in the world. They give Dresden its character as "Florence on the Elbe" and are the reason for city's reputation as one of the most beautiful in Europe.

Centre of Baroque Culture

He was Prince Elector of Saxony, King of Poland and Grand Duke of Lithuania, and his passion for building and collecting art made Dresden one of the leading political, economic and cultural centres of Europe. His legendary physical strength gave him the name Augustus the Strong (1670-1733), but he was even more notorious for his extravagant lifestyle. He and his court were responsible for many magnificent buildings that transformed the appearance of Dresden. Important collections of art and the first European porcelain factory were founded. Numerous artists and scientists came to the city, reinforcing its standing as a Baroque cultural metropolis.

Theaterplatz

The tour starts at this fine square, which is notable for its view of the famous buildings: from here you can enjoy a panorama taking in the opera house, royal palace, Zwinger, Hofkirche, the Italian Village and Neustädter Wache.

An equestrian statue of King John (1854-73) dominates the centre of the square. He already had a reputation as a scholar when he ascended the throne: he had published a translation of Dante's *Divine Comedy*.

Semperoper (opera house)

The opera house has survived fire, bombing and floods, and each time emerged again from ruins. Thanks to its imposing architecture and excellent acoustics, the opera house is famous across the world – in Germany it is known to millions as the iconic building, shown illuminated at night, in the advertisements for a well-known beer, Radeberger Pils.

When his first opera house fell victim to fire, Gottfried Semper designed a second theatre

(1871-78) in the style of the Italian High Renaissance. After its destruction in the war, this historic monument was rebuilt almost exactly as it originally was, but incorporating up-to-date stage technology, and ceremoniously reopened in 1985 with a performance of Carl Maria von Weber's *Der Freischütz*.

The focal point of the 84-metre-long semi-circular façade is the superb entrance with a quadriga of panthers. The interior design is even more impressive: vestibules and foyers with magnificent ceiling paintings and fine imitations of marble and wood lead to the elaborately decorated auditorium, a wonderful venue for evening performances with its chandeliers, rich adornments, royal box, sumptuous curtain and five-minute clock.

◆ *Theaterplatz 2*
Guided tours:
times at www.semperoper-erleben.de
or Tel. 0351/3207360

Altstädter Wache

Surrounded by Renaissance and Baroque architecture, the severe lines of a classical sandstone building in the form of an Ionic temple catch the eye in the south-east corner of the square. This is the former police station, which was built in 1830-32 to designs by the Prussian state architect Karl Friedrich Schinkel and now accommodates Visitor service of the Semperoper.

Italian Village

How should a Catholic monarch go about building a church in a predominantly Protestant country? Augustus the Strong solved the problem by giving the commission for his court church in 1739 to the Italian architect Gaetano Chiaveri, who brought his own craftsmen to Dresden with him. Almost two centuries later, in 1911-13, the director of public works Hans Erlwein closed off the square on the Elbe side by constructing a neo-classical sandstone building on the site where the Italian craftsman once lived - and the old name stuck.

»*Have a break*«
For Saxon cooking and Italian specialities, as well as historic painted decoration, go to the **Italienisches Dörfchen** ("Italian Village").
Theaterplatz 3 ◆ *from 10 am until 2 pm*

from 2 pm

Hofkirche (St Trinitatis Cathedral)
Schlossplatz 1
◆ *Mon-Tue 9am-6pm, Wed-Thu 9am-5pm, Fri 1-5pm, Sat 10am-9pm, Sun noon-4pm*
Guided tours: Mon-Thu 2pm, Fri-Sun 1pm

He was laid to rest in Cracow Cathedral, but his heart remained in Dresden! It was buried next to other rulers from the house of Wettin in the crypt of the imposing church that his son, Prince Elector Frederick Augustus II, commissioned the Italian architect Gaetano Chiaveri to build following the conversion of the Saxon court to Catholicism.

With its 90-metre-high bell-tower, the late Baroque church is one of the dominant sights on the city skyline and a counterpart to the Protestant Frauenkirche. The remarkable feature of the church interior is its unusual ground plan: in order not to provoke the ruler's Protestant subjects by holding Catholic processions out of doors, a processional way was built within the church around the nave.

Elbe valley
"From the high river bank I looked down on the wonderful Elbe valley that lay at my feet like a painting by Claude Lorrain ...", wrote Heinrich von Kleist of the stretch of countryside that is famous for its harmonious combination of nature and architecture, of city and landscape. The Elbe valley World Heritage site is almost 20 kilometres long, and extends from Schloss Übigau in the west to Schloss Pillnitz in the east, including parks

and gardens, the slopes of the valley and vineyards, palaces and old villages as well as the historic city centre.

While the exterior is richly decorated with figures of saints on the façade and balustrades, the interior is plain. One of its highlights is the *organ (1753) by the Saxon organ-builder Gottfried Johann Silbermann*, the only one of three in Dresden to have survived the Second World War. Take a look inside the Chapel of St John Nepomuk next to the main entrance, where there is a Pietà made of Meissen porcelain by the Dresden sculptor Friedrich Press (1973) in remembrance of the victims of the bombing on 13-14 February 1945.

Augustusbrücke
This bridge, one of Dresden's many landmarks, connects the historic heart of the Old Town (Altstadt) with the centre of the New Town (Neustadt). Since the late 13th century there had

been a bridge on this site. In the reign of Augustus the Strong it was replaced by an impressive new bridge designed by the Baroque architect Pöppelmann. However, as Pöppelmann's structure no longer met the requirements of modern shipping, in 1909 Wilhelm Kreis built a new one, consisting of nine arches of reinforced concrete, which spans the Elbe to this day.

Brühl Terrace

From Schlossplatz take the broad flight of steps that leads past the statues of the *Four Seasons* to "Europe's balcony", as the Brühl Terrace is called for its superb view of the cathedral, opera house, the Neustädter Ufer and the meadows on the river Elbe. In 1740 Frederick Augustus II made a gift of this part of the city fortifications to his minister of state, Henry, Count von Brühl, who ordered the construction of a Baroque pleasure garden with many buildings and held extravagant festivities here.

Today only the name remains from this time, and the 500-metre-long terrace has become a promenade, shaded by trees. Brühl's buildings were replaced in the late 19th century by monumental works of architecture such as the Ständehaus designed by Paul Wallot, architect of the Reichstag in Berlin, to serve as the chamber of the state parliament of Saxony from 1907. The neo-Baroque building known as the *Secundogenitur*, today part of the Hilton Dresden Hotel, was built for the second-born princes of the royal family.

»*Have a break*«
Enjoy the home-made cake and a wonderful view of the Elbe from the terrace of the **Vis-à-Vis** Café in the Hilton Dresden Hotel. ◆ 9am-6pm

until 3 pm

Steamers on the Elbe

If you would like to enjoy the view of the palaces and vineyards of the Elbe valley and the picturesque rocks of the Elbe sandstone mountains from the water, make time for a trip on the river. Since 1910 the world's largest and oldest fleet of paddle steamers has departed from its main quay below the Brühlsche Terrasse. The operator, Sächsische Dampfschifffahrt, has nine historic paddle steamers, which are more than 80 years old and ply the waters of the Elbe between Decin in Bohemia and Diesbar-Seusslitz. The traditional annual parade of steamers on 1 May in front of the Brühlsche Terrasse is a highlight of the year.

Tel. 0351/866090
www.saechsische-dampf-schiffahrt.de

3 Days in

from 3 pm

White Gold

A stele – made of Meissen porcelain, of course – in the Brühl Garden commemorates the man who invented porcelain, Johann Friedrich Böttger. As an apprentice apothecary he was allegedly able to turn silver coins into gold, which attracted the attention of King Frederick I of Prussia. The departure of the alchemist came to the ears of Augustus the Strong, who held him in Dresden. After several years of experiment Böttger and his collaborator, Ehrenfried Walther von Tschirnhaus, finally made a breakthrough in 1708: the result was not gold, but hard white porcelain, the basis for establishing the Meissen porcelain factory, the first in Europe, in 1710.

Kunstakademie

The eye-catching feature of the former Königliche Kunstakademie (royal academy of art) is the glass dome, which was christened "the lemon-squeezer" by locals on account of its ribbed structure. It is crowned by a gilded statue of Fama, the goddess of fame, and is the emblem of a building intended by the king to emphasise Dresden's status as one of the leading European cities of art and culture in the late 19th century. Today the four wings of this imposing structure, which is adorned with allegorical reliefs and statues, house a school for the fine arts.

Brühl Garden

To the east lies the plateau of the Jungfernbastion, on which Count von Brühl had a garden laid out. According to legend a hollow in the iron railing around the garden is the thumb-print of Augustus the Strong, who is said to have left this mark of his strength in between buying a painting, presiding over two state ceremonies and making love three times – however, the railing was not built until 14 years after his death.

Water still flows in the *Delphinbrunnen* (dolphin fountain), two sphinxes recall the now-vanished Belvedere, and a monument honours the famous Romantic painter Caspar David Friedrich, who lived in Dresden until his death.

Take a look inside the *synagogue* of coloured exposed concrete: its modern architecture is like a cube turned in on itself. The building's predecessor, built by Gottfried Semper, was destroyed in the night of pogroms in 1938.

Hasenberg 1

Fortifications

Between the Kunstakademie and the Albertinum a curving flight of steps leads past a bronze statue of Gottfried Semper to the entrance to the old fortifications, which lie beneath the Brühlsche Terrasse. Here you can explore the secret vaults of what is probably the oldest part of the city, dating from the Renaissance, and visit artillery courtyards, fortified chambers and the Ziegeltor, Dresden's last remaining city gate with the sentry posts for the soldiers who guarded the old city bridge.

www.festung-dresden.de
◆ *Sun-Fri 10am-6pm (April-Oct.), 10am-5pm (Nov.-March), Sat Guided tours every hour 10am-5pm*

Albertinum

The strange name comes from the man who commissioned the work: King Albert of Saxony had the old arsenal rebuilt in the late 19th century. Visitors come to the Albertinum not only for its architecture in the style of the Italian High Renaissance, but above all for its art collections. This refers to the *Skulpturensammlung* (sculpture collection), which possesses works from five millennia, such as the famous Dresden Boy, and the *Galerie Neue Meister*, one of the leading German museums of modern art with about 2500 works from the 19th and 20th centuries, including many German Romantic and Impressionist paintings and works by the world-famous Gerhard Richter. Following damage caused by the devastating floods of 2002, an auction held by more than 40 contemporary artists made it possible to present once again these collections, which represent a bridge between the past and the future.

www.skd-dresden.de ◆ *Tue-Sun 10am-6pm*

Black Stone

Wherever you look – the Zwinger, the palace and Hofkirche, the Brühl Terrace, even the Frauenkirche – black stone meets the eye. This is not soot remaining from war

destruction, as some people believe: since Dresden was almost completely reduced to rubble in 1945 and has largely been rebuilt since the war, the blackness of the stone cannot be a survival from those times. The explanation is simple: it is a patina, a natural colouring of the particularly hard Postaer sandstone, the result of oxidation of the iron in the sandstone. Over a period of time, this oxidation blackens the stone.

until 4 pm

3 Days in

from 4 pm

Treasures

The Frauenkirche and Green Vault

13 February 1945
When the sirens wailed at quarter to ten on the evening of Shrove Tuesday, and the people of Dresden headed for the cellars of their houses and apartment blocks, nobody realised the extent of what was to come: by noon the following day, in three closely spaced waves of attacks, British and American bombers had reduced the city to smouldering ruins. More than a million incendiary bombs started a firestorm that left behind a field of ruins covering 15 square kilometres and claimed the lives of 35,000 people.

The highlight of a walk though the old town is to visit the Protestant church, the pride of the people of Dresden, that once again crowns the skyline 60 years after its destruction. From here go on to the palace of the Wettin dynasty, where you can marvel at Europe's richest treasury.

Frauenkirche
Neumarkt
www.frauenkirche-dresden.de

♦ *10am-noon, 1-6pm*
(except during services and events)
Guided tours: Mon-Sat noon, Mon-Fri 6pm
Dome: Mon-Sat 10am-4pm, Sun 12.30-4 pm
(Nov.-Febr.), Mon-Sat 10am-6pm, Sun 12.30-6 pm
(March-Oct.)

When the bells rang out for the consecration of the new Frauenkirche (Church of Our Lady) on 30 October 2005, they marked the completion of an unparalleled commitment to reconstruction and a symbol of the reconciliation between nations: 45 years after this Baroque masterpiece was severely damaged as bombs rained down on 13 February 1945, and collapsed two days later, a group of committed citizens founded an initiative to rebuild the church, and publicised the idea around the world. They gained the support of 13,000 people in 23 countries – the son of a bomber pilot in London, for example, a skilled smith who made the cross for the tower – and raised over 100 million

1

euros, almost two-thirds of the costs of reconstruction.

Since then visitors from all over the world have flocked to the high interior of the church, which was designed by George Bähr.

Its special feature is the sandstone dome, the lower part of which has a concave form reminiscent of a bell. It weighs 12,000 tons, and its height of 24 metres and diameter of 26 metres make it the largest stone dome north of the Alps. Don't fail to go up to the viewing platform for a wonderful city panorama.

The interior of the octagonal building with its five galleries arranged in a semi-circle can hold 1,800 people and is a popular venue for concerts. The centre of attention is the richly decorated Baroque altar sculpted by Johann Christian Feige, depicting Christ on the Mount of Olives as its central scene. Look up at the underside of the dome, where eight pictures by the theatre painter Giovanni Battista Grone dating from 1734 – they depict the four evangelists and four Christian virtues – have been reconstructed.

Neumarkt
Until it was destroyed in 1945, the square around the Frauenkirche was regarded as an urban monument of the first order, representing the confidence and pride of the citizens of Dresden in the form of outstandingly fine Baroque townhouses. Since the reunification of Germany the restoration of these streets has been under way, taking account of modern requirements, in eight districts (Quartiere). The future appearance of the area can already be seen in the example of the Hotel de Saxe and in Quartier F, which has a hotel, restaurants and shops.

»*Have a break*«
From the terrace of the **Grand Café and Restaurant** in the Baroque Coselpalais you have a wonderful view of Dresden's landmark to accompany your coffee and cakes.
An der Frauenkirche 12 ◆ *10am-midnight until 4.45 pm*

3 Days in

from 4.45 pm

Residenzschloss (Royal Palace)
Hausmannsturm
◆ Wed-Mon 10am-6pm (mid-March-Oct)

From Neumarkt the tour continues to the magnificent residence of the Wettin dynasty, which developed over seven centuries from a castle, and following destruction in the war is now being rebuilt as a museum centre for the Free State of Saxony.

In Augustusstrasse, on the outside of the Langer Gang (long passage), look out for the famous Fürstenzug (procession of princes), the world's largest porcelain picture. Over a length of more than 100 metres, 25,000 tiles of Meissen porcelain portray Wettin rulers from 1127 to 1904 with their entourages. The Fürstenzug was created in 1872-76, originally in sgraffito, but as this quickly weathered, the design was then done on ceramic tiles.

Pass through the Georgentor, the first Renaissance building in Dresden, which like the rest of the palace complex was restored in neo-Renaissance style in 1900 on the occasion of the 800th anniversary of the ruling house. Then go to the Stallhof, one of the world's oldest tournament grounds. In past times spectators sat between the Tuscan columns of the arcade of the Langer Gang with its lovely 16th-century sgraffito façade.

In front of the tower named Hausmannsturm – from its viewing platform you can watch the building work in the palace grounds and the bustle of the old town in summer – note the bridge across which the Wettin rulers could reach the court church directly from the palace.

Kupferstichkabinett
(Collection of prints, drawings and photographs)

When a museum possesses more than 500,000 works on paper by over 11,000 artists from eight

centuries, then it can only display a fraction of its treasures at one time. And so the Kupferstichkabinett (print collection) puts on changing exhibitions, and allows visitors to admire originals by Dürer, Rembrandt, Caspar David Friedrich or Baselitz in the study room. All of this is on the same site where the Kupferstichkabinett, one of the world's oldest collections, was founded 450 years ago.

Taschenberg 2
Entrance: Sophienstrasse, 3rd floor
◆ Wed-Mon 10am-6pm
www.skd.museum/de

Grünes Gewölbe (Green Vault)
Entrance: Sophienstrasse or Kleiner Schlosshof
- *Neues Grünes Gewölbe Wed-Mon 10am-6pm*
- *Historisches Grünes Gewölbe Wed-Mon 10am-6pm*
Note: admission with timed tickets only
(Tel. 0351/49142000 or www.skd-dresden.de)

Unique works of art and superb examples of craftsmanship from the princely treasury are open to visitors in the west wing of the palace. They include the famous cherrystone in which 185 faces are said to be carved, and Johann Melchior Dinglinger's Baroque table-piece "Hofstaat zu Delhi" with 137 figures in gold and coloured enamel and 3,000 precious stones, for which Augustus the Strong paid 58,000 thalers (by way of comparison: it cost 50,000 to build Schloss Moritzburg without the decorations).

The room is called the Green Vault because it was once painted green before Augustus the Strong had it remodelled as a showcase for his jewels. On the ground floor the Baroque suite of the Historisches Grünes Gewölbe, with an incredible wealth of art on splendid tables and richly decorated, mirrored display walls, shows the magnificence that was once here. On the upper floor masterpieces from Europe's largest treasury can be seen behind glass in the Neues Grünes Gewölbe.

»Have a break«
Get in the mood for the evening in the **Karl May-Bar of the Taschenbergpalais**, which Augustus the Strong built for his mistress, Countess von Cosel.
Classic American Bar in Hotel Taschenbergpalais Kempinski Dresden, Taschenberg 3 ◆ *6pm-2am*

Armoury
When Albrecht the Bold established an independent duchy in the 15th century and made Dresden his city of residence, he also founded an armour chamber. Weapons for personal defence and tournaments, as well as the ceremonial weapons of the dukes and prince electors, were stored there. You can see the arms that the rulers collected after that time and the suits of armour that they wore in the Armoury, one of the world's most valuable collections of

ceremonial weapons and costumes. Thanks to the opening of the new giant hall the Rüstkammer collection has finally returned to the royal palace.

- *Residenzschloss, Entrance: Sophienstrasse or Kleiner Schlosshof, Wed-Mon 10am-6 pm, www.skd.museum/de*

until 5 pm

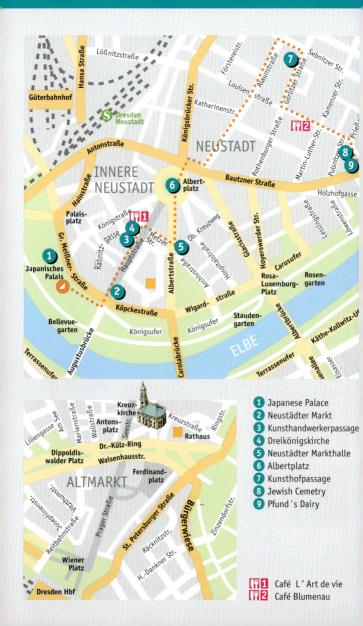

Day 2

Neustadt, strolling and shopping

The Neustadt (☓3h) 22
Strolling and Shopping (☓3h) 26

3 Days in

from 10 am

Baroque and the Colourful Republic
Neustadt - New Town

Spend the morning exploring and taking in the contrasts: stroll through the shopping streets of the Innere (inner) Neustadt, admire Baroque townhouses, chic boutiques and leafy courtyards, then take a walk through the Äussere (outer) Neustadt, a buzzing fashionable quarter.

Canaletto
... or Bernardo Bellotto (1722-80), to use the Venetian painter's real name, painted works that reveal today the appearance of Dresden in the Baroque period. As court artist to Prince Elector Frederick Augustus II he produced 14 views of Dresden with a photographic accuracy that still makes them of use to those restoring the buildings. His most famous view is "Dresden from the right bank of the Elbe below the Augustusbrücke"; it can be seen from the pavilion on the river path between the Japanese Palace and the Hotel Bellevue.

Japanese Palace
The district on the right bank of the Elbe is called Neustadt, New Town, because Augustus the Strong had the area previously known as Altendresden rebuilt as the "New Royal Town" after a fire in 1732. The four wings of the late Baroque and neo-classical palace built by Matthäus Daniel Pöppelmann to house Augustus the Strong's collection of Chinese, Japanese and Meissen porcelain is a testimony to this period. The name Japanese Palace derives from the curved form of the roof, reminiscent of the Far East, the Chinese herms in the courtyard and the Asiatic Atlas figures in the staircase.

Since the 18th century the building has been a MUSEUM USUI PUBLICO PATENS, a museum for the public benefit, as the inscription on the portico states. Today it houses three state museums: the museums of pre-history and ethnography, and the exhibition rooms of the natural history collections (see p. 56 f).

Neustädter Markt
On the Neustadt bridgehead of the Augustusbrücke the Baroque "Blockhaus", so called because of its cube-like shape, is the gateway to the district. Its correct name is Neustädter Wache, and it served as a customs house and checkpoint. The marketplace beyond it is dominated by a gilded *equestrian statue* of Augustus the Strong.

In the pose and dress of a Roman emperor, he directs his gaze towards his kingdom of Poland.

Hauptstrasse

The boulevard that leads north from here has long been one of the city's favourite shopping streets. The old plane trees in the middle of the road, the fountains and sculptures and the numerous shops and boutiques make it an attractive place to spend time window-shopping.

Take a look at the historic townhouses on the west side: here passageways and courtyards have been opened and connected to form the *Kunsthandwerker-* (craftsmen's) *Passage*. If you are interested in the works of Caspar David Friedrich, don't miss out on the Museum der Dresdner Romantik im *Kügelgenhaus*, which occupies the house of the Romantic painter Gerhard von Kügelgen (1722-1820).

Hauptstrasse 13
♦ *Wed-Sun 10am-6pm*
www.museen-dresden.de

On the corner of Metzerstrasse it is worth making a detour to the 19th-century *Neustädter Markthalle*, where fresh food and specialities are on offer on the stalls.

»Have a break«
For a cappuccino or more, **L'art de vie** in the back courtyard of the Societaetstheater with its charming garden is a pleasant place to sit at any time of day.
An der Dreikönigskirche 1a ♦ *10am-midnight until noon*

3 TIP Dreikönigskirche

Try to find a little time to visit the rebuilt Baroque Dreikönigskirche (Church of the Three Magi), which the church now uses as a place for meetings and events. Inside, the torso of the Baroque altar by Benjamin Thomae is a reminder of war damage, and below the organ gallery the twelve-metre-long Renaissance relief of the "danse macabre", which once adorned the Georgentor gate of the palace, refers to the transience of human life. From the top of the tower there is a beautiful view of the Neustadt district and the historic old town.

Hauptstrasse 23
♦ *Church 10am-6pm*
Tower:
Tue 11.30am-4pm
Wed-Sat 11am-5pm
Sun 11.30am-5pm
(March-Oct)
Wed noon-4pm
Thu-Fri 10am-4pm,
Sat 10am-5pm,
Sun 11.30am-4.30pm
(Nov-Feb)

3 Days in

from noon

Königstrasse

Königstrasse was built as a showpiece avenue connecting Augustus' porcelain palace with Albertplatz. Even today this exclusive street conveys an impression of how this part of Dresden once appeared. As the area was largely untouched in the bombing raids, the street with its adjacent alleys and passageways is now the only remaining Baroque residential and shopping quarter in the city.

Today high-class boutiques, antique shops, galleries and fine restaurants have found a home in the street. Take some time to visit the *Städtische Galerie für Gegenwartskunst* (city gallery of contemporary art), which provides up-to-the-minute insights into international and regional trends in contemporary art.

Kunsthaus Dresden, Rähnitzgasse 8,
www.kunsthausdresden.de
◆ Tue-Thu 2-7pm, Fri-Sun 11am-7pm

Albertplatz

In view of the streams of traffic it is hard to imagine that this was once the site of one of the most beautiful squares in the city, named after King Albert of Saxony (1873-1902). It is worth taking a look inside the neo-Baroque *Villa Eschebach* (1901), now the head office of the Volksbank Dresden, on the corner of Georgenstrasse.

The round temple at the end of Königsbrücker Strasse is part of the *Artesian Well*, which is supplied with water from a bore hole 234 metres deep on the opposite side of the street. Dresden's first *skyscraper*, an eleven-storey steel-framed construction by Hermann Paulick, stands at the north-west corner of the square, towards Antonstrasse.

Erich Kästner
"If it should be true that I not only know what is bad and ugly, but also what is beautiful, then I owe this gift to the good fortune of having grown up in Dresden", wrote Kästner, an author famous for children's books that were both humorous and critical of their times, in *When I Was a Little Boy* (1957). And so it was only natural that his home town should honour its famous son by erecting a monument that portrays the young Kästner sitting mischievously and happily on a wall. To find out more about his life and work, why not pay a visit the Erich Kästner Museum Dresden in Villa Augustin.

Antonstrasse 1,
▲ *Albertplatz,*
◆ Sun-Fri 10am-6pm

www.erich-kaestner-museum.de

Outer Neustadt

The area around Alaunstr., Görlitzer Str. and Louisenstr., where the Colourful Republic of Neustadt was founded in 1990, is no longer just the home of the alternative scene. With its many little shops, trendy pubs, bars and clubs the Äussere Neustadt is a vibrant quarter that is worth looking around, as the bombing of the last war largely spared its 19th-century architecture.

Don't miss the *Kunsthofpassage* between Alaunstr. and Görlitzer Str. It consists of five backyards,

thematically designed by Dresden artists, with shops and pubs that are interesting to view and visit. Take a side trip to Pulsnitzer Str. and Dresden's first *Jewish cemetery* (key in the Jewish cultural centre HATIKVA, Pulsnitzer Str. 19). From here go on to "the world's most beautiful dairy", the *Pfund's Dairy*. Countless tourists come to this shop, which sells milk, chocolate, cheese and soap, to admire its decoration of colourful art nouveau tiles by Villeroy and Boch.

Bautzner Strasse 79
▲ *Pulsnitzer Strasse*
♦ *Mon-Sat 10am-6pm,
Sun 10am-3pm*

»*Have a break*«
Café Blumenau is a rendezvous where the in-crowd and others come to talk over hot chocolate, home-made crepes and cocktails.
Louisenstrasse 67 ♦ *Mon-Thu 8.30am-midnight,
Fri 8.30-2am, Sat 9-2 am, Sun 9-midnight*

Colourful Republic of Neustadt

At the time of reunification, when Germany lost one republic, the foundation of a new one named Bunte Republik Neustadt was proclaimed in the New Town. In an attempt to lead a different way of life, punks, squatters and others from the alternative scene founded a state with its own currency, king, ministers and flag from 22 to 24 June 1990. Since the dissolution

of the provisional government of the district in 1993, a festival of the Bunte Republik (Colourful Republic) has been celebrated annually on the third weekend in June. It has mainly lost its political character and become a popular fair and festival of arts and culture.
www.brn-dresden.de

until 2 pm

from 3 pm

Around Altmarkt and Prager Strasse
Strolling and Shopping

Altmarkt is the ideal place to start a shopping tour from Prager Strasse to the main railway station. If you like, make a short detour from the shopping streets to see the oldest church in the city, the city hall, architecture from the Communist era of the German Democratic Republic (GDR) and 21st-century buildings.

Striezelmarkt
Every year tourists come from all over the world to one of Germany's oldest Christmas markets, which is named after an older version of Dresdner Christstollen cake. Of course the cake is on sale, as well as Pulsnitz spiced bread and mulled wine (Glühwein). Here, around the world's largest Christmas pyramid, stalls sell pottery from the Lausitz area, lace from Plauen and folk art from the Erzgebirge mountain region. The highlight of the Christmas fair is the Stollenfest, when historical figures, bakers and pastry-cooks parade from the Zwinger to the Striezelmarkt with a gigantic four-ton stollen.

www.striezel-markt.de

Around Altmarkt
The shopping trip starts at the old marketplace, which has been the centre of the city throughout its history. Of its original architecture, magnificent edifices in the Baroque and neo-Baroque styles, nothing remained in 1945 but a heap of ruins. The *Altmarkt-Galerie*, a modern shopping centre with more than 200 specialist stores and restaurants, is a particular attraction amidst the post-war buildings.

On the north side of the marketplace look out for the *Kulturpalast*, a flat 1960s steel-frame construction with a copper roof which is redevelloped at present. The mural entitled The *Way of the Red Flag* on the façade towards Schlossstrasse is a reminder of the art of the GDR.

In the *Kreuzkirche* (Church of the Cross), the city's oldest and largest place of worship, pause for a moment of quiet. The Baroque-style church, home of the world-renowned Dresden boys' choir, is famous for the sound of its 6,111-pipe Jehmlich organ. To view Altmarkt from above, there are two alternatives: either walk 256 steps up the church tower past Germany's second-largest peal of bells, or further east take the lift

up the tower of the *Rathaus* (city hall), which is topped by the figure of the Rathausmann. When events are held in the Rathaus, you can admire the art nouveau paintings by Otto Gussmann in the staircase leading to the public rooms.

Kreuzkirche, Altmarkt
◆ *Sun-Fri 10am-6pm, Sat 10am-3pm*
Rathaus tower, Kreuzstrasse
◆ *10am-6pm (May-Oct)*

Prager Strasse
Until 1945 it was Dresden's finest street for shopping and promenading, the link between the main railway station and the old town. In the 1960s it was rebuilt as a showcase quarter for the GDR and today, with its mixture of modern eastern-bloc and contemporary architecture, is considered an outstanding urban ensemble. For tourists and locals, however, it is principally a shopping street, as all the big brands and retail chains as well as well-known department stores are represented here. Shopping centres such as *Centrum Galerie*, *Prager Spitze* by the main station and the *Kugelhaus* on Wiener Platz – its glass ball (Kugel) a throwback to the world's first Kugelhaus,

built in Dresden in 1928 – round off the shopping experience.

Don't miss two contrasting works of architecture: the 1970s *circular cinema* on Prager Strasse with its five screens, and amidst the GDR concrete blocks the avant-garde multi-screen *Kristallpalast*, built in the shape of a distorted, sharp-edged, flowing glass crystal.

The Transparent Factory
With the assembly line for the Phaeton, Volkswagen has shown how to present automobile production as if on a stage: on the former exhibition grounds at the north-west corner of the Grosser Garten, pre-fabricated parts are manually assembled to make a luxury limousine behind 27,500 square metres of glass on three levels. Separated only by a wall of glass, visitors can look into the production facility, obtain information from a terminal about the assembly of the Phaeton and immerse themselves in the world of automobiles with the interactive drive simulator and car configurator.

Lennestrasse 1 (Pirnaische Vorstadt)
▲ *Strassburger Platz*
www.glaesernemanufaktur.de
Advanced booking required:
Tel. 0351/4204411

until 6pm

3 Days in

1. Alte Wache
2. New Palais
3. Water Palais
4. Lustgarten
5. Mountain P.
6. Charmillen
7. Camelia
8. Orangerie
9. Palm House
10. Chinese Garden

H1 Schloss Hotel Pillnitz

1. Blue Wonder Bridge
2. Leonhardi Museum
3. Schillerhäuschen
4. Luisenhof
5. Aerial Railway
6. Funicular Railway

H2 Villa Marie

1. Wallpavillon
2. Nymphenbad
3. Old Masters Picture Gallery
4. Glockenspielpavillon
5. Kronentor

Day 3

Schloss Pillnitz, Loschwitz and the Zwinger

Schloss Pillnitz (⏲2h) 30
Loschwitz (⏲2h) 32
The Zwinger (⏲2h) 34

3 Days in

from 10 am

Summer residence
Pillnitz Palace

Make an excursion to the summer residence of the Dresden royal court to find out how landscape and architecture can combine harmoniously, how many flowers can bloom on a camellia, and on which throne Augustus the Strong sat in state.

Museum of Arts and Crafts (Kunstgewerbemuseum)
Today the rooms of the Water Palace and Hill Palace accommodate the museum of arts and crafts (Kunstgewerbemuseum), which gives

an impression of life at the court of Saxony. In addition to the throne of Augustus the Strong, his unique silver furniture and Chinese-style lacquered furniture, the exhibits include works of art nouveau from Dresden, machine-made furniture from the Deutsche Werkstätte Hellerau and items by contemporary designers.

◆ *Tue-Sun 10am-6pm (May-Oct)*

Pillnitz Palace
August-Böckstiegel-Strasse 2
www.schlosspillnitz.de
▲ *Pillnitzer Platz,*
◆ *Park: 6-darkness*
◆ *Schloss: 10am-6 pm (Apr.-Oct.), Sat-Sun guided tour 11 am, noon, 2pm, 3 pm (Nov.-March)*

Even if visitors to Pillnitz no longer arrive in the style of court society, taking the princely gondola along the river Elbe and ascending steps flanked by sphinxes in order to enter the palace, the half-hour journey by bus through the Elbe valley to Pillnitz is still an experience in its own right. The palace and its grounds, which nestle into the landscape below the vineyards of the Elbe, are one of the most notable Baroque ensembles in Europe.

Augustus the Strong once made a gift of the palace to his mistress, Countess von Cosel, and took it away from her again when she fell out of favour. From 1720 he gave orders to his architect Matthäus Daniel Pöppelmann to remodel it as a residence in the so-called "Indian style", which meant Oriental or Far Eastern in the

Baroque period. With the double curve of its roofs, colourful chinoiserie paintings and Asiatic-looking decorations, the impressive *Water and Hill Palace* bear witness to the Baroque love of Chinese style.

About 100 years later the three neo-classical wings of the *New Palace* were built. With its Baroque elements it fits harmoniously into the ensemble. Today it houses an attractive exhibition on the history of the palace. A visit to the kitchens of the royal court is a fascinating glimpse into the catering arrangements for a royal court and the means of cooking and preserving food at that period. For a little peace and quiet go to the Catholic Chapel, which has a cycle of paintings on the life of the Virgin by the Nazarene school.

Take a walk in the 28-hectare *palace park*, which evolved over a number of generations and demonstrates the changing styles of landscape gardening with its hedge gardens from the time of Countess von Cosel, the English Garden and the Chinese Garden.

The Pillnitz Camelia

With a height of almost nine metres and a diameter of eleven metres, Camellia japonica L. is the botanical attraction of the palace gardens. When it flowers between mid-February and April, the camellia bears tens of thousands of crimson blooms. The plant is over 230 years old: it is reported to be the only survivor of four camellias that a Swedish botanist brought back from a journey to Japan in 1779. It was planted in its present position in 1801 and survived a fire in January 1905 without damage because the water used to extinguish the flames froze and protected it.

»Have a break«
Schloss Hotel Pillnitz is a good place to take refreshments at any time of year – in winter by a roaring fire, in summer on the terrace.
August-Böckstiegel-Strasse 10

until noon

3 Days in

from 12.30 pm

A blue wonder
Loschwitz

On this excursion you can explore the slopes of the Elbe valley, site of aristocratic villas, and discover the rural side of Dresden, which has a truly Mediterranean atmosphere in summer.

Albrechtsberg Palace
There is a wonderful view over the Elbe valley from the garden of the neo-classical palace that was built on the Loschwitz slopes by the Prussian court and state architect Adolf Lohse in the style of a Renaissance villa for Prince Albrecht of Prussia (1809-72). From the garden terrace, broad flights of steps lead to a semi-circular colonnade with pools, the Roman Bath. To find out more about the history of the palace and the life of Prince Albrecht of Prussia, take a look at the exhibition in the western gatehouse. Today the palace is used as a venue for events.

◆ *Exhibition:
10am-6pm,
free admission
Visits to the palace are possible only as a guided tour:
Tel. 0351/8115823
www.schloss-albrechtsberg.de*

If you have a little more time, stop on the way back at Körnerplatz in the old fishing and wine village of Loschwitz. "No-one could be happier than I now feel", wrote Caspar David Friedrich in his diary in 1803. Like many other artists of the Romantic period, Friedrich lived and worked here for a period. To this day the old centre of the village, with its lovingly restored houses of fishermen, wine-farmers and craftsmen, is a romantic place.

From the 18th century the vineyards of Loschwitz attracted wealthy nobles and artists, who built wine estates and summer residences here. If you take the three-minute trip up the hill with the *funicular railway* that dates from 1895 to the *Weisser Hirsch* (white stag), once a spa and now a place with fine houses, you can stroll through the narrow lanes and admire the magnificent villas. One of the best-known residents was Manfred von Ardenne, whose institute is still located here. To round off the trip don't fail to go to "Dresden's balcony", as the Luisenhof Restaurant (➤ p. 42) is known, to enjoy a superb view of the Elbe valley.

Other famous people have found their way to Loschwitz: the *Schillerhäuschen* commemorates Friedrich Schiller, who worked on his drama *Don Carlos* while visiting the vineyard house of the Körner family (Körnerstrasse 6): in the smallest museum in the city, pictures and manuscripts document

the works that Schiller wrote during his time in Dresden.

Schillerstrasse 19
◆ *Sat-Mon 10am-5pm*
www.stadtmuseum-dresden.de

Proverbs and ornamentation adorn the timber-framed building at Grundstrasse 26: the late Romantic painter, ink manufacturer and patron of the arts Eduard Leonhardi had it converted to artists' studios and named "Rote Amsel" (red blackbird). Today the *Leonhardi-Museum* has a permanent exhibition and shows works by contemporary artists.

Leonhardi-Museum
◆ *Tue-Fri 2-6pm*
www.leonhardi-museum.de

This tour finishes by crossing the river to Blasewitz by the Blue Wonder, as the Elbe bridge of Loschwitz is called on account of its pale blue paint. When the steel suspension bridge with a span of 140 metres was inaugurated in 1893, it was considered a great technical achievement.

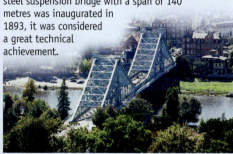

»Have a break«
In the idyllic beer garden of **Villa Marie** right by the Elbe below the Blaues Wunder, or in the Tuscan-style interior, you can enjoy the Italian side of Dresden.
Fährgässchen 1, Tel. 0351/315440,
◆ *Mon-Sat 11.30-1 am, Sun 10-1 am until 2 pm*

TIP: Aerial Railway

When Frederick Augustus, Crown Prince of Saxony, opened the world's first aerial cable railway on 6 May 1901 in the presence of a large crowd, it

was celebrated as a technical sensation. 385,000 persons used the railway in its first year of operation alone. The 274-metre-long system with its 33 supports transports passengers up to Oberloschwitz, which lies 84 metres higher. There is a wonderful view of the Elbe valley from the upper terminus. Next to the lower terminus stands the Baroque church of Loschwitz, which has been furnished with the Renaissance altar from St Sophia's church since being rebuilt.

Pillnitzer Landstrasse
www.dresdner-bergbahnen.de

from 3 pm

Old Masters and celestial globes
The Zwinger

Floods of 2002
When the tributaries of the Elbe became swollen after heavy rainfall in early August 2002 and the masses of water gradually exceeded the capacity of the reservoirs and overflow basins, the Elbe burst its banks. On August 17 in Dresden it reached an unprecedented level of 9.40 metres, which meant that the Zwinger, opera house and much of the city were under water and about 33,000 people had to be evacuated. Thanks to the untiring efforts of helpers from all over Germany and many donations in cash and kind, the damage was quickly repaired.

To round off a visit to Dresden, follow in the footsteps of the leisured court society in days of old by strolling on the terraces, admiring the fountains and listening to the glockenspiel. Inside the Baroque palace, world-famous collections of art await visitors.

Zwinger
Theaterplatz
▲ *Postplatz, Theaterplatz*
www.der-dresdner-zwinger.de
◆ *6am-10pm, free admission*

Desiring worthy surroundings for his court celebrations, Augustus the Strong gave his architect Matthäus Daniel Pöppelmann and his court sculptor Balthasar Permoser the task of creating a magnificent group of buildings. From 1709 they provided him with an ensemble of pavilions and galleries, symmetrically grouped around a courtyard, in which architecture, painting and sculpture fuse to form a single work of Baroque art. Today it is one of the greatest creations in Europe from this period.

As a result of its original position outside the city wall, the complex is called the Zwinger (bailey), even though it was no longer a fortification in the 18th century, but served as a garden and orangery, a place for Augustus' sumptuous festivities.

The main entrance is the *Kronentor*, one of the emblems of Saxony's capital city, which rises above the Long Gallery with its onion dome and Polish royal crown borne by four eagles. Pass

through into the great inner court to admire the fountains and the galleries lined with balustrades, figures and vases. It is possible to walk down the *Long Gallery*, which connects the gateway to the two *corner pavillons*, now home to the porcelain collection and the Mathematisch-Physikalischer Salon (➤ p. 57), and enjoy the view of the enchanting ensemble.

At the centre of the west arcade is the *Wallpavillon*, the architectural highlight of the Zwinger. It is crowned by a statue of Hercules with the globe, a reference to Augustus the Strong. A curving flight of steps leads up to the wall and further west to the Nymphenbad, one of the finest of all Baroque water features with its fountains, cascades and statues of nymphs. The *Glockenspielpavillon*, named after its famous glockenspiel, stands opposite as a mirror of the Wallpavillon.

Although the Zwinger today makes the impression of having been planned all of a piece, in fact the northern side was built over 100 years later. Between 1847 and 1854, on the side facing the Elbe, Gottfried Semper built the *Semperpavillon* that bears his name in the style of the Italian High Renaissance. Today it houses the gallery of paintings.

These glorious buildings lay in ruins after the bombing raid of 13 February 1945. Thanks to the determination of the people of Dresden, rebuilding of this masterpiece of Baroque architecture began in the same year and was completed in 1963.

Glockenspiel

If you always wanted to hear classical music played by a glockenspiel, make your way to the Glockenspielpavillon, where every hour on the hour and the half hour, and at quarter to and quarter past the hour, tunes that were composed especially for this instrument are played. From Easter to December at 10.15am, 2.15pm and 6.15pm, melodies by Bach, Vivaldi, Weber and others can also be heard. For this pavilion Pöppelmann planned a

glockenspiel consisting of 24 bells of Meissen porcelain, but the instrument was not built until the 1930s. Since its restoration in 1995, it has had 40 bells.

until 4 pm

3 Days in

from 4pm

Gemäldegalerie Alte Meister
(Old Masters Picture Gallery)
www.skd-dresden.de
♦ Tue-Sun 10am-6pm

The two angels at the bottom of the page have been reproduced millions of times and are probably more famous than the *Sistine Madonna* that Raphael painted for the high altar of the monastery church of San Sisto in Piacenza in 1512-13. The latter, one of the many masterpieces in the Gemäldegalerie, is among the most famous paintings of the Italian Renaissance. Over 50 years Augustus the Strong and his son Augustus III gathered together almost all the works for which the gallery is famous and for which Gottfried Semper designed the appropriate setting in 1854.

From Giorgione's *Sleeping Venus* to Titian's *Tribute Money*, the great artists of the Italian Renaissance are as much in evidence as the Flemish and Dutch masters of the 17th century. Vermeer's *Girl Reading a Letter at an Open Window* and Rembrandt's *Self-Portrait with Saskia* are just two of the highlights. Visitors can also see the works of German painters such as Dürer, Holbein and Cranach, of Murillo and other Spanish artists, and paintings by French masters such as Lorrain and Poussin, as well as the famous views of Dresden by Canaletto. The list of great works is lengthy: look forward to a fascinating tour through the history of European art!

Porcelain Collection
www.skd-dresden.de
♦ Tue-Sun 10am-6pm

With about 50,000 items of Chinese, Japanese and Meissen porcelain, the Dresden porcelain collection

---

"Make space for the great Raphael!"
Augustus III, Prince Elector of Saxony and King of Poland, is said to have spoken these words and to have pushed aside his throne with his own hands when the *Sistine Madonna* arrived in Dresden on 1 March 1754 after an eventful journey across the Alps on a horse-drawn cart. This may be a myth, but it is certain that the ruler had fulfilled a long-standing wish. He paid the astronomical sum of 60,000 thalers for the painting (compare this with Canaletto's annual salary of 12,750 thalers) and exerted political pressure to ensure that Duke Philip of Parma granted an export permit.

is one of the world's greatest museums of ceramics. The origin of the collection lay in Augustus the Strong's passion for the precious and fragile substance, which he himself described as "maladie des porcellaines". He founded the porcelain factory in Meissen and acquired expensive imports from China and Japan, but did not live to realize his dream of building a porcelain palace.

The treasures on view today include Chinese porcelain from the time of Kangxi, Japanese Imari and Kakiemon porcelain and items that trace the history of the Meissen manufactory. Among the best-known exhibits are the so-called dragoon vases, covered vases one metre in height with blue underglaze painting, for which Augustus the Strong paid not money but people: the price was 600 Saxon dragoons.

Mathematisch-Physikalischer Salon
www.skd-dresden.de
◆ Tue-Sun 10am-6pm

The tools and instruments that scholars used to make measurements in past centuries can be seen in the world-famous collection that originated in the prince electors' chamber of art and curiosities in 1560. From a 13th-century Arab globe of the heavens to Blaise Pascal's calculating machine of 1650, the clockwork representation of the planets' orbits that Eberhard Baldewein made for Elector Augustus around 1560 and a Russian wooden pocket watch made in the mid-19th century, there is much to marvel at here!

A Famous Mistress
Anna Constantia, Countess von Cosel (1689-1765), née von Brockdorf, was beautiful, intelligent and had a lively manner that enchanted Augustus the Strong, who made her the grande dame at his court. He even proposed marriage to her, and she bore him three children, but by interfering too much in political affairs she ended up spending 49 years of her life in imprisonment. When the Prince Elector of Protestant Saxony tried to regain the throne of Catholic Poland and converted to the Roman Catholic faith, he got tired of continual arguments and took a Polish Catholic mistress.

»*Have a break*«
After looking at all the art, you deserve a rest with coffee and cakes in the **Museumscafé Alte Meister.**
Theaterplatz 1a ◆ *from 11am until 5pm*

Service Hotels

From luxury hotels to hostels, there is a wide choice of accommodation in Dresden, with something to suit every taste. For information online, see: www.dresden-hotels.de.

Dresden Zoo

The landscaped zoo with its mature trees at the southern end of the Grosser Garten is a fine place to pass a few hours. Since its foundation in 1861 the zoo has been famed for its success in breeding orang-utans, especially since the story of the orang-utan Buschi, who was born on the voyage from Sumatra to Europe, made headlines around the world in the 1920s. Today the zoo is home to more than 2,000 animals of over 300 species and has an area of around 13 hectares. The highlights are the Africa House, the "zoo under the earth", which presents subterranean life, and the new lion savannah.

Tiergartenstrasse 1 (Seevorstadt-Ost)
www.zoo-dresden.de
▲ *Zoo*
◆ *8.30am-6.30pm (summer), 8.30am-4.30pm (winter)*

■ **ART'OTEL DRESDEN****
Ostra-Allee 33 (Old Town)
Tel. 0351/49220
Fax 0351/4922777
www.artotel.com
▲ Kongresszentrum

Everyone who appreciates modern architecture and art and likes good design has found the right address at this hotel in the heart of the historic old town.

■ **BACKSTAGE****
Hotel & MusicBar
Priessnitzstrasse 12 (Neustadt)
Tel. 0351/8887777
Fax 0351/8887799
www.backstage-hotel.de
▲ Diakonissenweg

Hotel on the edge of the new town in the restored old factory halls of Pfund's Dairy. The rooms have been individually designed by artists.

■ **BEST WESTERN MACRANDER HOTEL DRESDEN****
Buchenstrasse 10 (Neustadt)
Tel. 0351/8151500
Fax 0351/8151555
www.bestwestern.de
▲ Stauffenbergallee

A convenient location right in the middle of the new town.

■ **AIRPORT HOTEL DRESDEN****
Karl-Marx-Str. 25 (Klotzsche)
Tel. 0351/88330
Fax 0351/8833333
www.airporthoteldresden.de
▲ Flughafen

Four-star hotel near the airport, easy to reach but quiet and close to the Dresdner Heide nature reserve.

■ **DORINT HOTEL DRESDEN****
Grunaer Strasse 14 (Old Town)
Tel. 0351/49150
Fax 0351/4915100
www.dorint.com
▲ Deutsches Hygienemuseum

A modern four-star hotel between the Old Town and the Grosser Garten park.

Radisson SAS Gewandhaus

★ HILTON DRESDEN*****
An der Frauenkirche 5 (Old Town)
Tel. 0351/86420
Fax 0351/8642725
www.hilton.de/Dresden
▲ Altmarkt, Theaterplatz

Luxury hotel in the heart of the historic Old Town with a view of the Frauenkirche and the Elbe.

■ HOLIDAY INN DRESDEN****
Stauffenbergallee 25a (Neustadt)
Tel. 0351/81510
Fax 0351/8151333
www.holiday-inn-dresden.de
▲ Stauffenbergallee

First-class hotel conveniently located in the New Town on the edge of the entertainment quarter.

■ HOTEL AM TERRASSENUFER****
Terrassenufer 12 (Old Town)
Tel. 0351/4409500
Fax 0351/4409600
www.hotel-terrassenufer.de
▲ Synagoge

For non-smokers only, on the border of the historic Old Town with a wonderful view.

■ HOTEL BAYERISCHER HOF DRESDEN****
Antonstrasse 33-35 (Neustadt)
Tel. 0351/829370
Fax 0351/8014860
www.bayerischer-hof-dresden.de
▲ Dresden Neustadt

Stylish hotel in the New Town with an elegant room for balls and banquets.

■ HOTEL BÜLOW RESIDENZ DRESDEN
Rähnitzgasse 19 (Neustadt)
Tel. 0351/8003291
Fax 0351/8003100
www.buelow-residenz.de
▲ Bahnhof Neustadt, Neustädter Markt

Luxury hotel in the Baroque quarter. Its top-class restaurant, Caroussel, is one of the best in the country.

■ HOTEL ELBFLORENZ ****
Rosenstrasse 36 (Old Town)
Tel. 0351/86400
Fax 0351/8640100
www.hotel-elbflorenz.de
▲ Ammonstrasse/ Freiberger Strasse

First-class hotel directly adjoining the World Trade Center.

Grosser Garten
Dresden's green and leafy oasis occupies the site where once the Prince Elector of Saxony and his courtiers roamed through a Baroque pleasure garden and hunting ground. The park was landscaped in the English style in the 19th century, and is now an area of two square kilometres where you can stroll among Baroque sculptures, colourful flower beds, historic buildings such as the Baroque palais and idyllic spots with pools and ponds. To see rare and precious plants from all the continents of the earth, visit the Botanical Garden. And if you get tired, take a trip on the park railway.

▲ *Botanical Garden*

Service

Hotels

Dresden Exhibition Centre

The exhibition centre, Messe Dresden, has made its mark in architectural circles as a successful example of how to combine industrial architecture with the requirements of 21st-century business. The historic Erlwein'scher Schlachthof, once a slaughterhouse, has been converted to a site with four multi-purpose halls, several conference rooms, a roofed area of over 23,000 square metres and an open-air space of about 13,500 square metres, which is used each year for numerous fairs for specialists and the general public as well as for other events.

www.messe-dresden.de

■ **HOTEL KIPPING*****
Winckelmannstr. 6
(city centre)
Tel. 0351/478 500
www.hotel-kipping.de
▲ Hauptbahnhof, Bayrische Strasse

A privately run hotel in a beautifully restored neo-Renaissance villa in the city centre.

■ **HOTEL TASCHENBERG-PALAIS KEMPINSKI DRESDEN*******
Taschenberg 3 (Old Town)
Tel. 0351/49120
Fax 0351/4912812
www.kempinski-dresden.de
▲ Postplatz

Modern grand hotel in a rebuilt 300-year-old palais in the heart of the historic Old Town.

■ **MARITIM HOTEL DRESDEN******
Devrientstrasse 10-12/
Ostra-Ufer 2 (Old Town)
Tel. 0351/2160
Fax 0351/2161000
www.maritim.de
▲ Kongresszentrum

The hotel has been beautifully integrated into the historic Erlweinspeicher warehouse and is connected to the Congress Center by means of a subterranean passage.

■ **PULLMAN DRESDEN NEWA******
Prager Strasse 2 c
(Old Town)
Tel. 0351/4814109
Fax 0351/4955137
www.pullman-hotel-dresden.de
▲ Hauptbahnhof

The panoramic windows of this modern hotel on Prager Strasse provide a superb view of the city centre.

■ HOTEL MARTHA DRESDEN***
Nieritzstraße 11 (Neustadt)
Tel. 0351/81760
Fax 0351/8176222
www.hotel-martha-dresden.de
▲ Bahnhof Dresden-Neustadt

Quiet yet centrally located accommodation with a Christian tradition going back 100 years, in the city's only remaining Biedermeier-period street.

■ RAMADA RESIDENT HOTEL****
Brünner Strasse 11 (Laubegast)
Tel. 0351/25620
Fax 0351/2562800
www.h-hotels.com
▲ Alttolkewitz

This four-star accommodation near the Elbe between Pillnitz Palace and the Old Town is ideal for visitors who prefer to stay in a quiet place outside the city.

■ SCHLOSS HOTEL DRESDEN-PILLNITZ****
August-Böckstiegel-Strasse 10 (Pillnitz)
Tel. 0351/26140
Fax 0351/2614400
www.schlosshotel-pillnitz.de
▲ Schloss Pillnitz

Privately operated hotel in the palace grounds of Pillnitz, right by the river and surrounded by vineyards and orchards.

■ STEIGENBERGER HOTEL DE SAXE****
Neumarkt 9 (Old Town)
Tel 0351/43860
Fax 0351/4386888
www.steigenberger.com
▲ Pirnaischer Platz

A modern hotel on Neumarkt opposite the Frauenkirche. Its impressive façade is derived from the historic Hotel de Saxe (1786–1888).

Maritim Hotel Dresden

■ WESTIN BELLEVUE DRESDEN*****
Grosse Meissner Strasse 15 (Neustadt)
Tel. 0351/8050
Fax 0351/8051609
www.westinbellevuedresden.com
▲ Neustädter Markt

Luxury hotel amid picturesque gardens on the banks of the Elbe that command the famous "Canaletto view" of the Dresden skyline.

International Congress Center
The light and curvaceous architecture of the International Congress Center Dresden extends the famous Elbe silhouette westwards to the Marienbrücke. This state-of-the-art building, situated behind the parliament (Landtag) of the state of Saxony and directly connected to the Hotel Maritim by means of an underground passage, thus combining conference facilities with accommodation, has the latest technical equipment. Inside it holds up to 6,800 participants, and the Great Hall can be connected to neighbouring rooms for events with more than 4,000 persons.

www.dresden-congresscenter.de

Cafes and Lunch

If you need a break between sightseeing and shopping, there is no shortage of places in Dresden where you can sit down and take refreshments.

Dresden calendar

April
Dresden Film Festival:
www.filmfest-dresden.de/de/programm/programmstruktur
International Short-Film Festival:
www.filmfest-dresden.de/de/
Long Theatre Night:
lange-nacht-der-dresdner-theater.de

May
International Dixieland Festival:
www.dixielandfestival-dresden.com/de/
Karl May Festival:
www.karl-may-fest.de
Dresden Music Festival:
www.musikfestspiele.com

June
Republic of Neustadt:
brn-schwafelrunde.de
Gay Pride Week:
www.csd-dd.de
Dresden Long Night of Science:
www.literatur-jetzt.de
Elbe Slopes Festival:
www.elbhangfest.de

July
Dresden Palaces Night:
www.dresdner-schlössernacht.de
Film nights by the Elbe:
dresden.filmnaechte.de
Soap-box car race:
www.saloppe.de/SaloppeSeifen KistenRennen.htm

■ **AROMA-RESTAURANT**
Kreuzstrasse 3 (Old Town)
Tel. 0351/8212761
▲ Pirnaischer Platz
◆ Sun-Thu 9am-midnight
Fri-Sat 9am-1am

A delightful place for fans of Mediterranean food: a fine selection of bread baked in the oven, antipasta and some more ambitious dishes.

■ **CAFÉ-CENTRAL**
Altmarkt 5-6 (Altstadt)
▲ Altmarkt
◆ Mon 9am-9pm, Tue-Fri 9am-midnight, Sat 10am-midnight, Sun 10am-9pm

For the local specialities Eierschecke and Quark-käulchen, for brunch or afternoon coffee, this stylish café is a pleasant place to sit.

■ **CAFÉ KREUZTKAMM**
Altmarkt 25 (Old Town)
Tel. 0351/4954172
▲ Pirnaischer Platz
◆ Mon-Sat 9.30am-9 pm,
Sun noon-8pm

Traditional café that has been on Altmarkt since 1827.

■ **CAFÉ TOSCANA**
Schillerplatz 7 (Blasewitz)
Tel. 0351/3100744
▲ Schillerplatz
◆ 9am-7pm

Everyone who is tempted by cream gateau and other high-calory cakes will find a fine selection in this café.

■ **CAFÉ WIPPLER**
Körnerplatz 2 (Loschwitz)
Tel. 0351/2698040
▲ Körnerplatz
◆ Mon-Sat 6am-7pm,
Sun 8am-7pm

For Saxon Eierschecke or cream cakes, it's always worth stopping at this coffeehouse in Loschwitz.

■ **CUCHI**
Wallgässchen 5
(Prisco-Passage/Neustadt)
Tel. 0351/8627580
▲ Palaisplatz
◆ noon-3pm,
5.30pm-midnight

Fans of raw fish will like this sushi bar in the Prosco-Passage.

■ FALSCHER HASE
Rudolf-Leonhard-Str. 3 (Neustadt)
Tel. 0351/30959112
▲ Bischofsplatz
◆ Mon-Thu 4-10 pm, Fri-Sat noon-11pm, Sun noon-10pm

Dresden's first vegan restaurant, which serves cake as well as a BigSojaSteak-Burger and red lentil and coconut soup.

■ HOFCAFÉ
Görlitzer Straße 25/ Kunsthofpassage, Hof des Lichts (Äußere Neustadt)
▲ Görlitzer Strasse
◆ 10am-19pm (Apr.-Sep.), 11am-18pm (Oct.-Mar.)

Cake the way grandma baked it in what is probably Dresden's smallest coffeehouse.

■ LLOYD'S CAFÉ & BAR
Martin-Luther-Straße 17 (Neustadt)
Tel. 0351/5018774
▲ Pulsnitzer Straße
◆ Mon-Thu 8am-midnight, Fri 8-1am, Sat 9-1am, Sun 9am-7pm

For breakfast, aftenoon tea or pasta in the evening, Lloyd´s on Martin-Luther-Platz is beloved of early risers as well as night owls.

■ MAX ALTSTADT
Wilsdruffer Straße 24 (Altstadt)
Tel. 0351/48433870
▲ Postplatz
◆ Mon-Sat from 8am, Sun from 10am

Modern café with a sunny terrace where late risers can enjoy brunch or devote themselves straight away to Mediterranean snacks.

■ RESTAURANT CHIAVERI
in the Landtag (Saxon parliament)
Bernhard-von-Lindenau-Platz 1 (Old Town)
Tel. 0351/4960399
▲ Theaterplatz, Am Zwingerteich
◆ 11am-11pm

When the sun shines, the outdoor terrace is a fine place to enjoy a view over Dresden. When it rains, there are specialities from Saxony and the Mediterranean inside.

Dresden calendar

August
Dresden City Festival: *www.dresdner-stadtfest.com*
Laubegast Island Festival: *inselfest-laubegast.in-dresden.info*
Ostrale: *www.ostrale.de*
Dresden Summer Theatre: *www.sommertheater-dresden.de*
Dresden UrbanArt Festival: *www.lackstreichekleber.de*

September
Dresden Pottery Market: *www.toepfermarkt-dresden.de*

October
Dresden Bach Festival: *www.bachfest-dresden.de*
Dresden Jewish Week: *juedische-woche-dresden.de*

November
CYNETart: *www.cynetart.org*
Dresden Jazz Festival: *www.jazztage-dresden.de*
Festival of Contemporary Literature: *www.literatur-jetzt.de*
Mime Artists' Meet: *www.pantomimefestival-dresden.de*

December
Striezelmarkt (Christmas market): *www.dresden.de*
Advent celebration: *www.advenster.de*

Service

Restaurants

Whether you prefer Saxon potato soup or creamed foam of rocket with champagne, the restaurants of the capital of Saxony can serve up cuisine from all parts of the world.

Dresden's Vital Statistics

Dresden has around 525,000 residents, of whom 20,000 are not German nationals. The capital of the Free State of Saxony, which borders on Poland and the Czech Republic, lies in the south-east of the state on both banks of the Elbe between the foothills of the eastern Erzgebirge, the steeply sloping Lausitz granite region and the Elbsandsteingebirge (Elbe sandstone mountains).

Covering about 330 square kilometres, Dresden is Germany's fourth-largest city in terms of surface area. 36% of the area is devoted to buildings and roads, 2% is water, and 62% is woodland, park or countryside. This makes Dresden one of Europe's greenest cities.

A 30-kilometre stretch of the river Elbe passes through the city. The city boundaries have a length of 134 kilometres. The highest point in Dresden is at 383 metres, the lowest at 101 metres above sea level.

■ ALTE MEISTER
Theaterplatz 1a (Old Town)
Tel. 0351/4810426
▲ Postplatz
◆ from 11am

A museum café by day, and in the evening an unbeatable recommendation for all who enjoy creative cooking at moderate prices with a wonderful view of the opera house.

■ BEAN&BELUGA
Bautzner Landstrasse 32 (Weisser Hirsch)
Tel. 0351/4408800
▲ Plattleite
◆ Tue-Sat 6.30-10pm

A new star in Dresden's culinary heaven – this fine-dining restaurant is run by Germany's youngest Michelin-starred chef, Stefan Hermann.

■ CANALETTO
(in Hotel Westin Bellevue)
Große Meissner Straße 15 (Neustadt)
Tel. 0351/8051658
▲ Neustädter Markt
◆ Tue-Sat from 6pm

Here you can enjoy modern cross-over cuisine and the world-famous panorama at the same time.

■ CAROUSSEL
Rähnitzgasse 19 (Neustadt)
Tel. 0351/80030
▲ Neustädter Markt
◆ Tue-Sat from 6.30 pm

An elegant Baroque-style restaurant that is one of the best in the region. Chef Dirk Schröer has been awarded a Michelin star for his classic French food with a Mediterranean touch.

bean&beluga

■ FISCHHAUS ALBERTHAFEN
Magdeburger Strasse 58 (Friedrichstadt)
Tel. 0351/4982110
▲ Bahnhof Mitte
◆ 11am-11pm

Popular with lovers of seafood; right by the gates of the new exhibition centre.

Villandry

Sophienkeller im Taschenbergpalais

■ **HIERSCHÖNESSEN**
Görlitzer Str. 20 (Neustadt)
Tel. 0351/25652898
▲ Alaunplatz or Rothenburger Strasse
◆ Tue-Sat 6-11.30pm, Sun 6-10 Uhr

Nice restaurant at the Kunsthofpassage with summer garden and wine cellar, which cooks tasty according to the motto "Good taste is for sale".

■ **OGURA (HILTON)**
An der Frauenkirche 5 (Old Town)
Tel. 0351/4967390
▲ Altmarkt, Theaterplatz
◆ Tue-Sat 11.30am-2pm, Tue-Sun 5.30-10.30pm

Dresden's leading Japanese restaurant.

■ **RESTAURANT AND BAR LESAGE**
Lennéstrasse 1 (Pirnaische Vorstadt)
Tel. 0351/4204250
▲ Strassburger Platz
◆ Mon-Sat noon-3pm, Tue-Sat 6-10pm, Sun 11am-3pm

Lesage in the Glass Factory for VW cars is a place for luxury: upstairs the exclusive Phaeton is manufactured, downstairs gourmet meals are produced.

■ **SCHMIDT'S RESTAURANT**
Moritzburger Weg 67 (Hellerau)
Tel. 0351/8044883
▲ Am Hellerrand, Moritzburger Weg
◆ Mon-Fri 11am-2,30pm, 5.30-11pm, Sat 5-11pm

If you like unconventional cooking that lives up to the very highest standards, try this high-flying restaurant with a beautiful courtyard in the complex of the *Deutsche Werkstätten Hellerau*.

■ **SOPHIENKELLER AT TASCHENBERGPALAIS**
Taschenberg 3 (Old Town)
Tel. 0351/497260
▲ Postplatz
◆ 11am-1am

For an entertaining dining experience as in the days of Augustus the Strong, come to this old cellar restaurant where guests are greeted by characters in historic costume.

Villandry

■ **VILLANDRY – LUST AM ESSEN**
Jordanstrasse 8 (Neustadt)
Tel. 0351/8996724
▲ Louisenstrasse, Bischofsweg
◆ Mon-Sat from 6pm

Creative, Mediterranean-influenced food with a touch of subtlety in a highly praised restaurant in the heart of the trendy quarter.

Dresden is the cultural and economic capital of Saxony. In recent years it has become a highly-regarded and dynamic location for business and science, one of the top ten in Germany today. Companies working principally in the fields of microelectronics and electronics, information technology and biotechnology have been attracted to the area, taking advantage of the proximity of the university and many research institutes. The Transparent Factory, in which Volkswagen produces the luxury Phaeton car, has also boosted the local economy.

There are extremely close ties between research and industry, which is setting new standards of outstanding performance and innovation. At present the student population at the total of eight institutions of higher education and two academies amounts to more than 40,000 persons.

Tourism is a further important source of income for the city. Every year about 9,8 million visitors come to the capital of Saxony, 16 per cent of them from abroad.

Pubs and Beer Gardens

Whether you would like to bask in the southern European atmosphere of "Florence on the Elbe" or prefer to pass the evening in a pub that is full of character, you will find what you are looking for in Dresden.

A brilliant advertising idea

... occurred to Hugo Zietz, who named his cigarette and tobacco factory Yenidze, after the area of tobacco cultivation in Turkey, and commissioned Martin Hammitzsch in 1907 to build a factory in the style of a mosque. Today hardly anyone realises that the building with the colourful dome, Moorish tiles and elements of art nouveau decoration is really a steel-frame construction and that the minaret contains a chimney. Hammitzsch was expelled from the national chamber of architects for his design, but Zietz went on to become a leading player in the tobacco industry. And since then, the Baroque panorama of Dresden has had an Oriental touch.

■ BLUE NOTE CLUB & BAR
Görlitzer Strasse 2b
(Äussere Neustadt)
▲ Görlitzer Strasse 2b
◆ 8pm-5am

A small jazz club and bar with fantastic live music. See www.jazzdepartment.com for the programme.

■ FELDSCHLÖSSCHEN-STAMMHAUS
Budapester Str. 32
(Wilsdruffer Vorstadt)
Tel. 0351/4718855
▲ Budapester Strasse
◆ from 11am

In the engine hall of this former brewery, a protected monument, a wide range of hearty dishes are served and washed down with refreshing Feldschlösschen beer. Good Health!

■ FISCHHAUS
Fischhausstrasse 14
(Albertstadt)
Tel. 0351/899100
▲ Fischhausstrasse
◆ Mon-Fri noon-midnight, Sat 11am-midnight, Sun 11am-11pm

For a wonderful beer garden and traditional food it is worth making a trip out to the historic tavern on the edge of the Dresdner Heide area.

■ KUPPELRESTAURANT IN DER YENIDZE
Weisseritzstrasse 3
(Friedrichstadt)
Tel. 0351/4905990
▲ Maxstrasse
◆ noon-11pm

In the highest beer garden or beneath the dome, guests at Yenidze have a view over the roofs of Dresden while enjoying international and Saxon culinary treats.

★ PUROBEACH CLUB
Leipziger Str. 15b
(Pieschen Süd)
Tel. 0351/7952902
▲ Hafenstrasse
◆ From 11am (summer)

Holiday atmosphere at the Neustädter harbour with everything a sun-lover could wish for: a beach, deck chairs, and cocktails.

■ RAUSCHENBACH-DELI
Weisse Gasse 2 (Old Town)
Tel. 0351/8212760
▲ Pirnaischer Platz
◆ From 9am

This combination of coffee bar, bistro and restaurant is a great place for a rendezvous – for breakfast, after shopping or for a cocktail in the evening.

■ RED ROOSTER
Rähnitzgasse 10 (Neustadt)
Tel. 0351/2721850
▲ Räcknitzhöhe
◆ from 5pm

Dresden's oldest pub attracts whisky-drinkers with over 100 single malts and blends from Scotland, as well as Irish whiskey.

■ SCHILLERGARTEN DRESDEN
Schillerplatz 9 (Blasewitz)
Tel. 0351/811990
▲ Schillerplatz
◆ 11am-1am

A trip to the Blue Wonder is always rewarding – whether you want to order Saxon potato soup, Vienna schnitzel or just a glass of Feldschlösschen pils in the winter garden or in the beer garden on the Elbe. To get there you can either ride a bike, board a steamer or just catch a tram.

■ TORWIRTSCHAFT
Lennèstrasse 11 (Pirnaische Vorstadt)
Tel. 0351/4595200
▲ Strassburger Platz
◆ from 11am

A popular beer garden in the Grosser Garten with seats for 800 under the spreading trees.

■ WATZKE BALL-& BRAUHAUS
Kötzschenbroder Strasse 1/ Ecke Leipziger Strasse (Pieschen)
Tel. 0351/852920
▲ Altpieschen
◆ 11am-midnight

In the shady beer garden with the famous Canaletto view try a glass of the pils brewed on the premises, and don't forget to have a look inside one of the loveliest ballrooms in Saxony.

Dresden Specialities

Dresdner Sauerbraten:
Beef marinated in buttermilk, juniper berries, bay-leaves and cloves, browned in honey and cooked in the marinade.

Eierschecke:
Pastry base with sweet quark cream, covered in a mixture of eggs, butter and sugar.

Fettbemme:
Dripping with apple and marjoram on fresh black bread.

Glitscher:
Potato fritters made from grated raw potato, flour and egg, served with sugar and apple sauce.

Krautwickel:
Leaves of white cabbage filled with minced meat, heart and diced smoked meat.

Quarkkeulchen:
Dough made of potatoes, flour, eggs, raisins and quark, fried until golden brown and sprinkled with cinnamon and sugar.

Service

Bars & Nightlife

Whether you want to round off the evening with a drink or prefer an energetic session on the dance floor, Dresden offers everything you need.

"A rarity. Wines from Saxony."

… is the claim of Germany's smallest wine region. Vines have been cultivated for over 800 years in the Elbe valley from Pirna to Dresden, Radebeul and Meissen and in the idyllic wine villages around Diesbar-Seusslitz. There are now about 20 producers in the area,

and many who make wine as a hobby. They grow Müller-Thurgau, Riesling, Pinot Blanc, Pinot Gris and Traminer grapes on the slopes of the valley, where the mild climate and excellent soil produce dry wines that are fruity and full-bodied with pleasant acidity. You can try them direct from the growers, in wine bars, at autumn wine festivals and in a "Strausswirtschaft", a temporary tavern open in the wine season.

■ **BAR 84**
Alaunstr. 66 (Neustadt)
Tel. 0173/4127787
▲ Albertplatz, Louisenstrasse
◆ Mon-Sat from 7pm

In this bar with the legendary red settee you have to make a choice between 200 different cocktails.

■ **BAR IM STEIGENBERGER HOTEL DE SAXE**
Neumarkt 9 (Old Town)
Tel. 0351/43860
▲ Pirnaischer Platz
◆ 10am-1am

A classic bar with piano music: the ideal hang-out for an after-work drink, aperitif or digestif.

■ **BLAUER SALON**
(im Parkhotel Dresden)
Bautzner Landstrasse 7 (Neustadt)
Tel. 0351/4848799
▲ Plattleite
www.blauersalon.com

The salon where splendid festivities and balls were held in the 1920s is today one of the city's most fashionable addresses for partying.

■ **BLUE NOTE CLUB & BAR**
Görlitzer Strasse 2b (Outer Neustadt)
Tel. 0351/8014275
▲ Louisenstrasse
◆ 8pm-5am

Blue Note has cult status among nightowls thanks to a wide range of music from modern jazz to swing, soul and punk.

art'otel Dresden

■ **DOWNTOWN**
Katharinenstrasse 11-13 (Neustadt)
Bahnhof Neustadt
Tel. 0351/8115592
www.downtown-dresden.de

Chill out or dance: Dresden's oldest club has two dance floors and three bars.

- **FRANK'S BAR**
Alaunstrasse 80
(Outer Neustadt)
Tel. 0351/65888380
▲ Bischofsweg
♦ from 6pm

Classic bar serving about 200 different cocktails.

- **KATYS GARAGE**
Alaunstrasse 48
(Outer Neustadt)
Tel. 0351/6567701
www.katysgarage.de
▲ Bischofsweg

M 5 Nightlife

This in-club with a GDR Trabant car on the roof has a varied programme that appeals to old and young alike, with music from Abba to Zappa for the over-30s, and the Neustadt dance evening on Saturdays.

- **M.5 NIGHTLIFE**
Münzgasse 5 (Old Town)
Tel. 0351/4965491
▲ Pirnaischer Platz
♦ Thu-Sat from 9pm

Not a club for teenies, but a club and bar for late-nighters with an open-air cocktail bar on the terrace.

- **PIER 15**
Leipziger Strasse 15b
(Pieschen Süd)
Tel. 0351/41884699
www.pier15.de
▲ Hafenstrasse

Fashionable party venue in the historic warehouses of the Neustädter harbour with a varied programme of events.

- **TWIST-SKYBAR**
(in Innside Dresden)
Salzgasse 4 (Old Town)
Tel. 0351/795150
▲ Synagoge
♦ 8pm-2am

Here you can sip a cocktail with a view of the Frauenkirche.

Dresden Music Festival
Every year in spring visitors from all over the world come to Dresden to listen to classical music in combination with other genres – jazz, dance, film, literature and visual arts – at famous and less-known venues, in unconventional locations and in the open air. Since its foundation in 1978 the Dresden Music Festival has been one of the world's leading festivals for classical music. Under the motto "Empire", in 2013 world-famous orchestras, ensembles and soloists are staging encounters with the the sound worlds of the musical island England.

www.musikfestspiele.com

Wellness

Visitors to Dresden who would like to indulge body and soul with a little relaxation after a meeting or a shopping trip will find a wide choice of places where they can take a sauna, have a massage or some other healing therapy or go for a swim in a natural pool: there is something to suit every taste.

The "Saxon Switzerland"
A romantic landscape that attracts many tourists with its great flat-topped mountains, crags and cliffs, deep gorges and bizarrely shaped rock walls originated in the seas of the Cretaceous period. This 360-square-kilometre area of the Elbe sandstone mountains was christened "Saxon Switzerland" by the Swiss painters Adrian Zingg and Anton Graff, whom it reminded of the Jura mountains when they went walking there in 1766. The medieval towns make a visit worthwhile even if you are not interested in hiking or climbing.

www.saechsische-schweiz.de

■ **AUSZEIT**
Arndtstrasse 7
(Radeberger Vorstadt)
Tel. 0351/6465497
www.auszeit-dresden.de
▲ Waldschlösschen

Take time out here for physical and mental relaxation with a Hawaiian temple massage or a Thai or Tibetan sound massage.

Elbamare Erlebnisbad Dresden

■ **ELBAMARE ERLEBNIS-BAD DRESDEN**
Wölfnitzer Ring 65
(Gorbitz Ost)
Tel. 0351/410090
www.elbamare.de
▲ Merianplatz
◆ 10am-10pm

The Elbamare is a great place to swim, tone up or chill out, with massage jets and a geyser in the pool, a warming jacuzzi, saunas and a rest area beneath the glass dome.

■ **GEORG-ARNHOLD-BAD**
Helmut-Schön-Allee 2
(Seevorstadt)
Tel. 0351/4942203
www.dresdner-baeder.de
▲ Queralle
◆ 9am-7pm (summer)

1700 square metres of water surface in a centrally located swimming pool next to the football stadium and the Grosser Garten.

■ **HAMAM AL SULTAN**
Wiener Strasse 44
(Südvorstadt)
Tel. 0351/4519708
www.hamam-dresden.de
▲ Zoo
◆ 11am-10pm

Oriental health and beauty with a sauna, steam bath, pool and massage in the Villa de Baron, a historic monument.

■ **SPA LOUNGE**
(in the Hotel Taschenbergpalais Kempinski Dresden)
Taschenberg 3 (Old Town)
Tel. 0351/4912870
www.kempinski.com/de/dresden/hotel-taschenbergpalais/luxus-spa/
▲ Postplatz
◆ 6.30am-10pm

In the pool, the sauna, the gym or a massage, here you can forget everyday cares.

Hilton Dresden

Maritim Hotel Dresden

■ **MARIENBAD WEISSIG**
Am Marienbad 12 (Weißig)
Tel. 0351/2683366
▲ Hermann-Löns-Strasse
◆ 10am-7pm (summer)

A 6000-square-metre bathing lake with a gondola pond in the countryside on the border of the Dresdner Heide area – a wonderful place to relax in good weather.

■ **NORDBAD DRESDEN**
Louisenstrasse 48
(Outer Neustadt)
Tel. 0351/8032360
www.nordbad-dresden.de
▲ Bautzner Strasse, Rothenburger-Strasse, Louisenstrasse
◆ Sauna: Mon 9am-10pm (women), Tue 9am-noon (men) noon-10pm (mixed), Wed 2-10pm, Thu-Fri 9am-10pm, Sat-Sun 10am-8pm

This temple to the bathing cult is over 100 years old. Plunge into the swimming pool, take a Finish sauna or relax in the steam bath.

■ **SCHWEBEBAD DRESDEN**
Schützenplatz 14 (Old Town)
Tel. 0351/4400127
www.schwebebad-dresden.de
▲ Bahnhof Mitte
◆ Mon-Sat 10am-10pm

Here you can drift in peace in the salt-water floating tank first, and complete the process of relaxation afterwards with a massage.

■ **PURE SPA HILTON**
An der Frauenkirche 5
Tel: 0351/40761952
www.spa-wellness-dresden.de
▲ Altmarkt, Theaterplatz
◆ 10am-10pm

Wether massage or body treatment, here you can spoil yourself from head to toe.

Schwebebad Dresden

■ **WALDBAD WEIXDORF**
Zum Sportplatz 1a
(Weixdorf)
Tel. 0351/8804164
www.waldbad-weixdorf.de
▲ Weixdorf (Rathenaustrasse, Gleisschleife)
◆ 10am-8pm (summer)

Swim in the natural surroundings of the Weixdorf lake or hire a boat and stay dry.

Radebeul
Villa Shatterhand, residence of a popular author of Western stories, Karl May, is now a museum and just one of many sights in this picturesque little town among the vineyards of the Lössnitz district. On the weekend of Ascension Day an annual festival is held in honour of Karl May. If you are more interested in the traditions of the Saxon Wine Route, the municipal wine estate Hoflössnitz or Schloss Wackerbarth, the estate of the state of Saxony, are the right addresses. The wines taste good all year round, not only at the autumn festival in the historic village of Altkötzschenbroda on the last weekend in September.

www.radebeul.de

Service

Culture

Dresden has a legendary reputation as a city of music. The opera attracts visitors from far and wide, and the Palucca school of dance has world renown. Theatre, cabaret and revues, too, make Dresden an exciting place for a cultural trip.

Saxon State Orchestra, Dresden

Richard Wagner called it a "magic harp"; Richard Strauss, who arranged for nine of his operas to be premiered by the Saxon State Orchestra (Sächsische Staatskapelle Dresden) and dedicated his Alpine Symphony to them, thought it "the best opera orchestra in the world". Since its foundation in 1548 by Prince Elector Moritz of Saxony, the Staatskapelle has performed continuously for over 450 years and has always been a first-rate ensemble under the leadership of famous conductors such as Heinrich Schütz, Carl Maria von Weber and Karl Böhm. Its repertoire ranges from Baroque music to contemporary pieces. In addition to performances at the Dresden opera house, the orchestra plays all over the world under its principal conductor Christian Thielemann.

www.staatskapelle-dresden.de

Music & Dance

■ **ALTER SCHLACHTHOF**
Gothaer Strasse 11
(Leipziger Vorstadt)
Tel. 0351/431310
www.alter-schlachthof.de
▲ Hafenstrasse, Grossenhainer Platz

Popular concert venue. Well-known pop and rock musicians perform here.

■ **DRESDNER PHILHARMONIE**
Tel. 0351/4866866
Program and venues under:
www.dresdnerphilharmonie.de

Under its principal conductor Michael Sanderling the Philharmonie is one of Germany's leading ensembles and has been the concert orchestra of the Saxon capital since 1870.

■ **DRESDNER SINFONIKER**
Tel. 0351/4903605
Programme and venues:
www.dresdner-sinfoniker.de

An award-winning young symphony orchestra that has a modern style and performs contemporary music, including world premieres.

■ **FESTSPIELHAUS HELLERAU**
Karl-Liebknecht-Strasse 56 (Hellerau)
Tel. 0351/8833700
www.festspielhaus-hellerau.com
▲ Heinrich-Tessenow-Weg

The seat of the Hellerau European Art Centre. The programme includes theatre, dance, performance art and music, including the Dresden Festival of Contemporary Music.

■ **HOCHSCHULE FÜR MUSIK CARL MARIA VON WEBER**
Wettiner Platz 13
(Altstadt)
Tel. 0351/4923600
www.hfmdd.de
▲ Bahnhof Mitte

A wide variety of concerts are held in the school of music – with free admission.

■ **JAZZCLUB NEUE TONNE**
in the basement of the Kulturrathaus Dresden
Königstrasse 15 (Neustadt)
Tel. 0351/8026017
www.jazzclubtonne.de
▲ Albertplatz

An institution for jazz-lovers in Dresden, featuring the JazzDD series, jam sessions and concerts by

international stars of the jazz world.

■ **KREUZKIRCHE**
An der Kreuzkirche 6 (Altmarkt)
Tel. 0351/4965807
www.dresdner-kreuzkirche.de
▲ Pirnaischer Platz

In the church you can hear not only the world-famous Kreuzchor but also organ concerts and a varied programme of other musical offerings.

■ **SEMPER KLEINE SZENE**
Bautzner Str. 107 (Neustadt)
Tel. 0351/4911705
www.semperoper.de
▲ Nordstrasse

This is the studio theatre of the main opera house (Semperoper), devoted to contemporary and forward-looking musical theatre. It also stages performances and workshops for children.

■ **SEMPEROPER**
Theaterplatz 2 (Old Town)
Tel. 0351/4911705
www.semperoper.de
▲ Postplatz

One of Europe's most famous opera houses, home of the Saxon State Orchestra Dresden, the world's oldest orchestra with a continuous existence, and the Semperoper ballet ensemble.

■ **STAATSOPERETTE DRESDEN**
Pirnaer Landstrasse 131 (Laubegast)
Tel. 0351/2079999
www.staatsoperette-dresden.de
▲ Altleuben

One of the few European stages for light operetta that puts on not only works of Viennese operetta but also those of other composers and musicals.

Theatre and Cabaret

■ **BOULEVARD THEATER DRESDEN**
Maternistrasse 17 (Wilsdruffer Vorstadt)
Tel. 0351/26353526
www.boulevardtheater.de
▲ Josephinenstrasse

New theatre for entertainment culture and folk theater in Dresden.

■ **CARTE BLANCHE THEATER**
Priessnitzstrasse 10 (Radeberger Vorstadt)
Tel. 0351/204720
www.carte-blanche-dresden.de
▲ Diakonissenkrankenhaus

Revues like the Lido and Moulin Rouge in Paris.

■ **HERKULESKEULE**
Sternplatz 1 (Altstadt)
Tel. 0351/4925555
www.herkuleskeule.de
▲ Josephinenstrasse

Satirical political cabaret, one of the best ensembles of this kind in Germany. For German-speakers.

Carl Maria von Weber (1786-1826)
A statue on Theaterplatz commemorates the man who made the newly built Dresden opera house one of the leading venues in Germany. While Weber was in Dresden he wrote *Der Freischütz*, which earned him a place in music history as the founder of German national opera. He was born in Eutin in Holstein and had piano and singing lessons at an early age, as his father intended him to be a child prodigy. He composed his first piece at the age of nine but was not destined to have a long career, dying shortly after the premiere of his opera *Oberon* in London.

Culture

Kreuzchor
In the age of hip-hop and rap, the choir boys of the Kreuzchor, heirs to a centuries-old tradition of choir music, are something special. The original purpose of the choir, which started as a school of Latin attached to the Kreuzkirche church, was to perform sacred music at church services and vespers. Today the wide-ranging repertoire encompasses early Baroque works, Bach cantatas and modern choir music. The boys of the Kreuzchor have sung in churches and concert halls all over the world – a fame they owe to Rudolf Mauersberger, their director of music from 1930 to 1971, who undertook many tours abroad with the choir.

www.kreuzchor.de

■ **KABARETT BRESCHKE & SCHUCH**
Wettiner Platz 10
(Wilsdruffer Vorstadt)
Tel. 0351/4904009
www.kabarett-breschke-schuch.de
▲ Bahnhof Mitte

Excellent satirical cabaret in the former state printing works of Saxony.

■ **KLEINES HAUS**
Glacisstrasse 28 (Neustadt)
Tel. 0351/4913555
www.staatsschauspiel-dresden.de
▲ Albertplatz, Rosa-Luxemburg-Platz

Second stage for the state theatre company in a former pub and ballroom. Mainly contemporary works.

■ **COMÖDIE DRESDEN**
Freiberger Strasse 39
(in the World Trade Center/Old Town)
Tel. 0351/866410
www.comoedie-dresden.de
▲ Freiberger Strasse

The theatre for those who don't take drama too seriously: farces, comedies, revues.

■ **MERLINS WUNDERLAND**
Zschonergrundstrasse 4
(Kemnitz)
Tel. 0351/4219999
www.merlins-wunderland.de
▲ Zschonergrundstrasse

A "dining experience", combining culinary and cultural delights.

■ **PROJEKTTHEATER**
Louisenstr. 47
(Outer Neustadt)
Tel. 0351/8107600
www.projekttheater.de
▲ Bautzner/Rothenburger Strasse

Independent communication centre for experimental and mixed-genre off-theatre.

■ **SCHAUSPIELHAUS**
Theaterstrasse 2 (Old Town)
Tel. 0351/4913555
www.staatsschauspiel-dresden.de
▲ Postplatz

Home of the Dresden state theatre ensemble and the largest theatre auditorium in the city, staging a high-quality programme of classical and contemporary drama. The theatre upstairs is an established venue for matinees, readings and concerts.

■ **SOCIETAETSTHEATER**
An der Dreikönigskirche 1a
(Neustadt)
Tel. 0351/8036810
www.societaetstheater.de
▲ Albertplatz, Neustädter Markt

A small theatre, Dresden's oldest. Drama, puppet theatre of various kinds and dance feature heavily on the programme.

■ **THEATERKAHN– DRESDNER BRETTL**
Terrassenufer an der Augustusbrücke (Old Town)
Tel. 0351/4969450
www.theaterkahn-dresden.de
▲ Theaterplatz

Performances of the works of Heinrich Heine, Erich Kästner and others are the attractions at an evening on an old barge on the Elbe.

■ **THEATERRUINE**
Königsbrücker Platz (Hechtviertel)
Tel. 0351/2721444
www.theaterruine.de
▲ Tannenstrasse

In summer the ruins of St Pauli Church are a stage for theatre, concerts and events.

■ **1001 MÄRCHEN GMBH**
Weisseritzstrasse 3 (Friedrichstadt)
Tel. 0351/4951001
www.1001maerchen.de
▲ Maxstrasse

A wonderful place for the young and the young-at-heart who like to listen to a fairy tale.

Kinos

■ **FILMTHEATER SCHAUBURG**
Königsbrücker Str. 55 (Neustadt)
Tel. 0351/8032185
www.schauburg-dresden.de
▲ Bischofsweg

Cult cinema from the Golden Twenties. In addition to films, regular concerts, readings and film festivals are staged.

■ **THALIA. COFFEE AND CIGARETTES**
Görlitzer Str. 6 (Neustadt)
Tel. 0351/6524703
www.thalia-dresden.de
▲ Görlitzer Str./Nordbad

Award-winning arthouse cinema, Dresden's smallest.

■ **UFA - KRISTALLPALAST DRESDEN**
St. Petersburger Strasse 24a (Old Town)
Tel. 0351/4825825
www.ufa-dresden.de
▲ Walpurgisstrasse

Multi-screen cinema with out-of-the-ordinary architecture.

Gret Palucca and the Art of Dance

Dresden has a tradition of dance: in 1911 Jacques-Dalcroze founded a training academy for rhythmic gymnastics and education that was described by his pupil, Mary Wigman, as "the cradle of modern expressive dance". She was the

teacher of Gret Palucca, one of the leading exponents of expressive dance, who founded a school in 1925 that placed intellectual and artistic education on a par with the purely physical dance training. This tradition is continued in Germany's only independent school of higher education for dance, which offers courses in stage dance, choreography and dance teaching, as well as a course of study with master classes.

www.palucca.eu

Service

Museums

Hygiene and transport, prehistory and the history of the city: the museums of Dresden are a voyage of discovery through many centuries and fields of knowledge.

Moritzburg

Not far from Dresden, in a forested area rich in wildlife with many lakes, stands a castle with four strong round towers which Augustus the Strong commissioned Matthäus Daniel Pöppelmann to convert into a pleasure palace and hunting lodge. Many visitors come to Moritzburg to see the original furnishings in the state apartments, which have largely survived, and the 200 rooms of the palace. The Baroque leather wall coverings are unique, and the collection of hunting trophies is one of the best in Europe.

◆ 10am-5.30pm (April-Oct), Tue-Sat 10am-4.30pm (Nov.-March)

www.schloss-moritzburg.de

■ **ALBERTINUM**
➤ p. 15

■ **BUCHMUSEUM**
Zellescher Weg 18
(Südvorstadt Ost)
www.slub-dresden.de
▲ Staats- u. Universitätsbibliothek
◆ 10am-6pm

Treasures of the art of books, including the Dresden Maya manuscript and Albrecht Dürer's sketchbook.

■ **CARL-MARIA-VON-WEBER MUSEUM**
Dresdner Straße 44
(Pillnitz)
www.stmd.de
▲ Van-Gogh-Straße
◆ Wed-Sun 1-6pm

Exhibition about the life and work of the composer Carl Maria von Weber (1786-1826).

■ **DEUTSCHES HYGIENE-MUSEUM**
Lingnerplatz 1
(Seevorstadt Ost)
www.dhmd.de
▲ Deutsches Hygiene-Museum
◆ Tue-Sun 10am-6pm

A museum about humanity that has seven rooms, each devoted to a different aspect of human life.

■ **ERICH KÄSTNER-MUSEUM**
➤ p. 24

■ **GEMÄLDEGALERIE ALTE MEISTER**
➤ p. 36

■ **GRÜNES GEWÖLBE**
➤ p. 19

■ **KUNSTGEWERBEMUSEUM**
➤ p. 30

■ **KUPFERSTICHKABINETT**
➤ p. 18

■ **LANDESMUSEUM FÜR VORGESCHICHTE**
Japanese Palace
Palaisplatz 11
(Neustadt)
www.voelkerkunde-dresden.de
▲ Palaisplatz
◆ Tue-Sun 10am-6pm

Changing exhibitions with objects from the ethnographic collection, which has over 90,000 items from all parts of the earth.

■ **LEONHARDI-MUSEUM**
➤ p. 33

■ **MATHEMATISCH-PHYSIKALISCHER SALON**
➤ p. 37

■ **MILITÄRHISTORISCHES MUSEUM DER BUNDESWEHR**
Olbrichtplatz 2
www.mhmbw.de
▲ Olbrichtplatz, Stauffenbergallee/
◆ Mon 10am-9pm, Tue, Thu-Sun 10am-6pm

This exhibition on over 800 years of German military history in the new building by Libeskind.

■ **MÜNZKABINETT**
in the Hausmannsturm of the Residenzschloss
www.skd-dresden.de
▲ Theaterplatz (Old Town)
◆ Wed 10am-5.30pm

Collection of Saxon coins and medals from important periods in the history of the Saxon state; plus orders, historic shares, etc.

■ **MUSEUM DER DEUTSCHEN ROMANTIK**
➤ p. 23

■ **MUSEUM FÜR SÄCHSISCHE VOLKS-KUNST MIT PUPPEN-THEATERSAMMLUNG**
Jägerhof, Köpckestraße 1 (Neustadt)
www.skd-dresden.de
◆ Tue-Thu 10am-6pm

In addition to folk art from Saxony, the museum has a historic collection devoted to puppet theatre.

■ **PORZELLANSAMMLUNG**
➤ p. 36

■ **RÜSTKAMMER**
➤ p. 19

■ **SCHILLERHÄUSCHEN**
➤ p. 32

■ **STAATLICHES MUSEUM FÜR VÖLKERKUNDE**
Japanese Palace
Palaisplatz 11 (Neustadt)
www.voelkerkunde-dresden.de
▲ Palaisplatz
◆ Tue-Thu 10am-6pm

State museum of ethnography – 280,000 years of Saxon history.

■ **STAATLICHE NATUR-HISTORISCHE SAMM-LUNGEN DRESDEN**
in the Japanese Palace
Palaisplatz 11 (Neustadt)
www.snsd.de
▲ Palaisplatz
◆ Tue-Thu 10am-5pm

State collection on natural history, including dinosaurs and geology.

■ **STADTMUSEUM DRESDEN**
Wilsdruffer Straße 2 (Old Town)
www.stmd.de
▲ Pirnaischer Platz
◆ Tue-Thu, Sat-Sun 10am-6pm, Fri 10am-7pm

The history of Dresden from the foundation of the city to the present day.

■ **STÄDTISCHE GALERIE FÜR GEGENWARTSKUNST**
➤ p. 24

■ **VERKEHRSMUSEUM IM JOHANNEUM**
Augustusstraße 1 (Old Town)
www.verkehrsmuseum-dresden.de
▲ Pirnaischer Platz, Theaterplatz
◆ Tue-Sat 10am-6pm

One of the oldest museums of technology in existence. Many original vehicles and valuable models representing all means of transport.

Die Brücke
Thanks to four students of architecture – Ernst Ludwig Kirchner, Fritz Bleyl, Erich Heckel and Karl Schmidt-Rottluff – the city of Dresden was the source of decisive impulses in the development of classic modern art. Coming together in 1905 as the founders of a group known as "Brücke" (bridge), they rejected the traditional academic style of painting and searched for new modes of artistic expression. Their work made Dresden the birthplace of German Expressionism: disregarding the established canons of painting, they employed luminous colours and simplified forms to express their feelings.

Service

shopping

Meissen porcelain, Dresden Christstollen or Christmas decorations from the Erzgebirge region: in Dresden you will not be at a loss when buying souvenirs!

Dresdner Christstollen
The famous cake has been baked at Christmas for centuries in a shape representing the infant Christ in swaddling clothes. Dresden Christstollen has been known since about 1400, although it was originally called "Striezel" – hence the name Striezelmarkt (see p. 26). Christstollen owes its special taste to papal intervention: as the use of butter, milk and other fine

ingredients was not permitted during the Advent period of fasting, and Christstollen made only from flour, yeast and water tasted boring, Prince Elector Ernest of Saxony asked Pope Nicholas V to lift the ban on using butter. The pope consented – on condition that in penance a payment was made for the building of Freiberg cathedral.

■ **BAUMSTRIEZEL MANUFAKTUR**
Alaunstrasse 25 (Outer Neustadt)
▲ Görlitzer Strasse
◆ Mon-Sat noon-7pm, Sun 2-6pm

Here you can buy the Baumstriezel in sweet or savory varieties.

■ **BLUE CHILD**
(in the KunsthofPassage)
Görlitzer Strasse 25 (Outer Neustadt)
▲ Bischofsweg
◆ Mon-Fri 11am-7.30pm, Sat 11am-4pm

For bibliophiles and lovers of paper and calligraphy: decorative papers, paper lamps, pens and much more.

■ **BUNZLAUER KERAMIKLADEN**
Bautzner Strasse 81 (Outer Neustadt)
▲ Diakonissenkrankenhaus
◆ Mon-Fri 10am-5pm, Sat 10am-4pm (March-Dec), Mon-Fri 10am-4pm, Sat 10am-2.30pm (Jan-Feb)

Come here to buy beautiful pottery decorated in deep blue from Boleslawiec in south-western Poland.

■ **CAFÉ KREUTZKAMM**
Alter Markt 25 (Old Town)
▲ Prager Strasse
◆ Mon-Sat 9.30am-9pm, Sun noon-6pm

A favourite place to buy genuine Dresden Christstollen and other sweet treats.

■ **CAMONDAS SCHOKOLADEN**
An der Frauenkirche 20 (Old Town)
▲ Pirnaischer Platz
◆ Mon-Th 10am-8pm, Fri-Sat 10am-10pm, Sun 10am-6pm

Come here to buy the most delicious chocolates by the world's best producers.

■ **KUNSTSTUBE „AM GOLDENEN REITER"**
Hauptstrasse 17 (Neustadt)
▲ Neustädter Markt
◆ Mon-Fri 10am-7pm, Sat 10am-4pm

Here it's Christmas all year round, with an enormous selection of wooden items from the Erzgebirge for the tree and the nativity scene.

■ **MEISSENER PORZELLAN AM FÜRSTENZUG**
An der Frauenkirche 5 (in Hotel Hilton/Old Town)
▲ Pirnaischer Platz
◆ Mon-Fri 9.30am-7pm, Sat-Sun 9.30am-6pm

Porcelain and figurines from the famous factory in Meissen.

■ **LOUISDOOR**
Louisenstraße 4 (Outer Neustadt)
▲ Louisenstraße
◆ Mon-Fri 10am-noon, 1-7pm, Sat 10am-2pm

Toys or environmentally friendly children's clothes – here you find attractive and useful gifts.

■ **DRESDNER PORZELLAN AN DER FRAUENKIRCHE**
Neumarkt 7 (Old Town)
▲ Altmarkt, Theaterplatz
◆ Mon-Sat 11am-7pm, Sun noon-6pm

Hand-made and hand-painted porcelain from the Sächsische Porzellan Manufaktur Dresden, a source of quality craftsmanship since 1872.

■ **WEINKONTOR**
(in the Altmarktgalerie/Basement)
Webergasse 1 (Old Town)
▲ Altmarkt, Postplatz, Dr.-Külz-Ring
◆ Mon-Sat 10am-9pm

If you have no time to drive along the Saxon Wine Route, come here to buy Saxon wine and spirits.

Patents from Dresden
... are no rarity. In 1892 Robert Sputh invented the so-called wooden felt board, a forerunner of the beer mat, by pouring paper pulp into round moulds and drying it (patent no. 68499). Only a year later Karl August Lingner, a Dresden businessman, launched Odol mouthwash. In 1895 Christine Hardt registered a patent

for an early version of the bra, described as a "women's bodice with breast supports" and consisting of handkerchiefs connected to adjustable men's braces. The coffee filter, too, comes from Dresden: Melitta Benz patented it in 1905 as no. 347895.

Addresses

SG Dynamo Dresden
Dynamo Dresden sports club, founded on 12.04.1953 as a police sports association, was one of the most successful and popular football clubs of the German Democratic Republic. Before unification in 1990, Dynamo won the championship eight times and the cup seven times. After unification, the club played in the first Bundesliga division for five years, but was then relegated to the regional league as a result of its hopeless financial position and loss of Bundesliga licence. Following a period of consolidation, in which the club was twice cup-winner in Saxony, since 2011 the black-and-yellows played in the second division of the Bundesliga again for two years, were relegated once more, and were promoted back to the second division in 2016.

www.dynamo-dresden.de

■ **INFORMATION**
DRESDEN TOURISMUS GMBH
Prager Straße 2b
01069 Dresden
Tel. 0351/501501
Fax 0351/501509
www.dresden.de
TOURIST-INFORMATION at the Frauenkirche
Neumarkt 2
◆ Mon-Fri 10am-7pm, Sat 10am-6pm, Sun 10am-3pm
in Central Station
8am-8pm

■ **BANKS**
◆ Banks in Dresden are normally open from 9am to 4pm on weekdays.
◆ In the main station: Reisebank Dresden Hauptbahnhof: 8am-9pm

■ **RAIL TRAVEL**
DEUTSCHE BAHN
Tel. 0180/6996633
www.bahn.de

■ **DRESDEN AIRPORT**
Tel. 0351/8810
www.dresden-airport.de

■ **TICKET SALES (CONCERTS, THEATRE ETC)**
Tourist Information,
Hauptbahnhof or Neumarkt 2
Tel. 0351/501501
Florentinum,
Ferdinandstrasse 12,
Tel. 0351/866600
Schillergalerie,
Loschwitzer Str. 52a,
Tel. 0351/315870
www.konzertkasse-dresden.de
SAX Ticket, Königsbrücker Strasse 55 (Schauburg),
Tel. 0351/8038744
www.saxticket.de
Haus an der Kreuzkirche,
An der Kreuzkirche 6
Tel. 0351/4965807

■ **MEDIA**
Print: Sächsische Zeitung (SZ), Dresdner Neueste Nachrichten (DNN), Dresdner Morgenpost (Gruner und Jahr), Bild-Zeitung, Dresdner Kulturmagazin, Sax, Sächsischer Bote, Wochenkurier
Radio: MDR, Radio PSR, Radio Energy (NRJ), Radio Dresden und R.SA
Television: MDR, Dresden Fernsehen

■ **CAR RENTAL**
Avis, Tel. 01806/217702
Europcar,
Tel. 040/52018 8000
Hertz, Tel. 01806/003688
Sixt, Tel. 01806/252525

■ **PUBLIC TRANSPORT**
Dresdner Verkehrsbetriebe AG
Service telephone:
0351/8571011
www.dvb.de

For 24 or 48 hours, three or five days, the **Dresden City Card** gives you free travel on buses, trams and trains, free admission to the museums of the Dresden State Art Collections, many price reductions on city tours and boat trips, exhibitions, museums and theatres, and discounts in restaurants and shops. You can buy the **Dresden City Card** at the tourist information offices in Schössergasse 23 or central station and in the customer centres of the public transport system.

■ **EMERGENCY NUMBERS**
Police: 110
Fire brigade: 112
Emergency doctor: 116117
Emergency dentist:
www.zahnarzt-notdienst.de
ADAC breakdown service: 01802/222222

■ **CITY TOURS**
AUGUSTUSTOURS E.K.
Guided bike tours along the Elbe cycle path.
Turnerweg 6
01097 Dresden
Tel. 0351/56348 20
www.augustustours.de
BREY KUNST KULTUR
Königstraße 12
01097 Dresden
Tel. 0351/3745419
www.brey-kunstkultur.de
HOP ON/HOP OFF BUS TOUR
A double-decker bus tour lasting 90 minutes. Ticket-holders can get off and on again at any of the 22 stops.

▲ Theaterplatz/An der Augustusbrücke
www.stadtrundfahrt-dresden.de
IGELTOUR DRESDEN
Löwenstr. 11
01099 Dresden.
Tel. 0351/8044557
www.igeltour-dresden.de
Tours with Fräulein Kerstin
Kerstin Klauer-Hartmann
Kamenzer Straße 29
01099 Dresden
Tel. 0351/8019048
www.stadtfuehrung-dresden.de
VISIT DRESDEN
Birgit van Stipriaan
Bayreuther Str. 30
01187 Dresden
Tel. 0173/3536600
www.visit-dresden.de

■ **TAXI**
Tel. 0351/211211
www.taxi-dresden.de
LIMOUSINEN- & CHAUF-FEURSERVICE 8X8 AG
Tel. 0351/8888888
www.8mal8.de

■ **INTERNET**
In English:
www.germany-tourism.de
www.dresden.de/index_en.php
www.dresden-tourist.de
www.skd.museum.de
In German:
www.besuchen-sie-dresden.de
www.dresden-neustadt.de
www.dresden-online.de
www.dresden-und-sachsen.de

The Saxon dialect
... is not just the way that people speak in and around Dresden, but also an essential basis for the High German language. Because Saxony was a prosperous region in the Middle Ages where people from all parts of the German-speaking world lived, a lingua franca known as Meissen Chancellery German was developed that was soon understood in all

almost parts of the Holy Roman Empire. This is the reason why, for example, Luther translated the Bible into Saxon, which helped to establish the dialect increasingly as the standard version of German.

Dresden's History

1089	Henry I becomes Margrave of Meissen, rule of the House of Wettin begins.
1206	First written mention of Dresden.
1403	Charter granting city rights to the part of Dresden on the right bank of the Elbe (Altendresden).
1485	The brothers Ernest and Albert divide Saxony between them; the residence of Albert's branch of the family is in Dresden.
1539	Reformation in Dresden.
1547	Duke Moritz receives the title of Prince Elector; Saxony becomes the leading Protestant state in Germany.
1549	Dresden and Altendresden merge.
1685	A great fire destroys almost all the buildings in Altendresden.
1694	Frederick Augustus I (Augustus the Strong) becomes Prince Elector.
1697	Augustus the Strong converts to Catholicism and becomes King Augustus II of Poland.
1709	Johann Friedrich Böttger discovers the recipe for making porcelain; a year later the Meissen porcelain factory is founded.
1710	Start of construction work on the Zwinger; 1726 on the Frauenkirche.
1733	Augustus the Strong dies and is succeeded as Prince Elector by his son Frederick Augustus II.
1806	French troops occupy Dresden. The city becomes capital of the Kingdom of Saxony, a state created by Napoleon.
1831	First constitution of Saxony.
1838	Start of construction of the first Semperoper (opera house).
1849	Bloody repression of the Dresden May rebellion.

1862	The first German cigarette factory starts production in Dresden.
1901	The world's first suspended rail system goes into operation in Loschwitz.
1905	The association of Expressionist artists known as "Brücke" is founded.
1918	Abdication of the King of Saxony; Dresden becomes capital of the Free State of Saxony.
1945	From 13 to 15 February the city is bombarded by Allied warplanes and destroyed to a large extent. At least 35,000 people lose their lives.
1952	Abolition of federal states and reorganisation of regional government in the GDR. Dresden becomes a regional capital.
1965	The Zwinger is the first historic building to be restored and reopened.
1978	"Dresden Music Festival" takes place for the first time.
1985	Rebuilding of the Semperoper (opera house) completed.
1989	Peaceful revolution: in Dresden and elsewhere the end of the GDR begins.
1990	After reunification Dresden becomes capital of the newly founded Free State of Saxony.
2002	Devastating floods in many parts of the city.
2004	The Neues Grünes Gewölbe, in 2006 the Historisches Grünes Gewölbe, are open for visitors again.
2005	Inauguration of the rebuilt Frauenkirche.
2006	Dresden is proclaimed City of Science and celebrates its 800th anniversary.
2013	The Waldschlößchenbrücke is opened.
In 2015	Dresden received the Europe Prize from the Committee of Ministers of the Council of Europe.

Index

Albertinum 15
Albrechtsberg Palace 32
Altmarkt 26
Altstädter Wache 10
Armoury 19
Augustus the Strong 3, 10, 12, 14, 19, 22, 34, 35, 36, 37
Augustusbrücke 12
Bars 48 f.
Beer gardens 46 f.
Blue Wonder 33
Brühl Terrace 13, 15
Cafés 42 f.
Canaletto 3, 4, 22
Carl Maria Weber 3, 11, 53
Countess von Cosel 19
Culture 52 ff.
Die Brücke 57
Dreikönigskirche 23
Dresden Exhibition Centre 40
Dresdner Christstollen 4, 58
Dresdner Music Festival 49
Dynamo Dresden 60
Erich Kästner 5, 24
Fortress Dresden 15
Frauenkirche 4, 15, 16
Frederick August II 3, 11, 13
Fürstenzug 18
Gottfried Semper 3, 10, 35
Green Vault 19
Großer Garten 39
Hofkirche 10, 12, 18
Hotels 38 ff.
International Congress Center 41
Italian Village 10, 11
Japanese Palace 22
Kreuzkirche 26, 54
Kulturpalast 3, 26
Kunstakademie 14
Kupferstichkabinett 18
Loschwitz 3, 32 f.,
Lunch 42 f.
Mathematisch-Physikalischer Salon 35, 36
Matthias Daniel Pöppelmann 22, 30, 34, 35
Meissener Porzellan 14
Moritzburg 56
Museum of Arts and Crafts 30
Museums 56 f.
Neumarkt 17
Neustädter Markt 22
Neustadt 3
Nightlife 48 f.
Old Masters Picture Gallery 36
Outer Neustadt 3, 11, 25
Paddle steamers 3, 4, 13
Pfund's Dairy 25
Pillnitz Palace 12, 30
Porcelain Collection 35, 36
Prager Straße 27
Pubs 46 f.
Raphael 4, 36
Restaurants 44 f.
Royal Palace 10, 15, 18
Saxon Switzerland 50
Saxon State Orchestra Dresden 52
Semperoper 4, 10
Shopping 58 f.
Striezelmarkt 26
Synagogue 3, 15
Theaterplatz 10
Transparent Factory 3, 27, 45
Wellness 50 f.
Yenidze 46
Zwinger 3, 10, 15, 34 f.

Picture Credits

All photos BKB Verlag except Alte Meister 37 be., André Wirsig/Amt für Kultur und Tourismus Radebeul 47 Mi.r., 48 Mi.l., 51 be., art'otel dresden 40 be.r., 48 Mi.r., bean&beluga 44 ab., Dresden Marathon 43 be., Dresden Tourismus GmbH/Christoph Münch U1 be.r., 13 Mi.r. 14 Mi.ab., 16 ab.l., 17 Mi.r., 26 Mi., be., 27 be., 31 Mi.be., 32 Mi., 34 be., 39 be., 56 Mi.l., Dresden Tourismus GmbH/Frank Exß 2 be., 21, Dresden Tourismus GmbH/Sven Döring 4-5, 7.ab., Dresden Tourismus GmbH/Sylvio Dittrich 6-7 be., 11 Mi., 14 ab.r., 26 ab.r., 47 ab., 58 Mi., Elbamars Erlebnisbad Dresden 50 Mi., Elisabeth Heinemann/Dresdner Musikfestspiele 49 Mi., Eva Winkler, MVD 56 Mi.r., Fotolia 2-3 ab., Frauenkirche/Jörg Schöner 1, Herkuleskeule 55 ab., Hilton Dresden 40 ab., 41 ab., 50 be., Holiday Inn Dresden 45 be., Hotel Am Terrassenufer 39 ab., Hotel Elbflorenz 39 Mi., Hotel Taschenbergpalais Kempinski Dresden 40 Mi., Komödie Dresden 53 ab., Kreuzchor 54 ab., M 5 Nightlife 49 be., Maritim Hotel Dresden 51 ab., Matthias Creutziger 10 ab.r., Pullman Dresden Newa 27 ab.Mi., Messe Dresden GmbH 40 be.l., Oe's Gastronomie GmbH 46 be., Palucca Schule Dresden – Hochschule für Tanz 55 Mi., Radisson SAS Gewandhaus 38, Schlösserland Sachsen/www.schloesserland-sachsen.de 30 Mi.r., Schwebebad Dresden 51 Mi., Semperoper 52-53 o., SG Dynamo Dresden e.V. 60 l., Sophienkeller im Taschenbergpalais 45 ab., Staatliche Kunstsammlungen Dresden, Gemäldegalerie Alte Meister/Hans-Peter Klut 36 Mi., Staatliche Kunstsammlungen Dresden, Gemäldegalerie Alte Meister/Hans-Peter Klut /Elke Estel 19 Mi. ab., 36 ab.r., be., 37 Mi., Staatliche Kunstsammlungen Dresden,Kupferstich-Kabinett/Herbert Boswank 18 Mi.l, Staatliche Kunstsammlungen Dresden, Grünes Gewölbe 19 ab.r., Staatliche Kunstsammlungen Dresden, Grünes Gewölbe/Jürgen Karpinski 19 Mi.be., Staatliche Kunstsammlungen Dresden, Kunstgewerbemuseum/Jürgen Karpinski 4, Staatliche Kunstsammlungen Dresden, Porzellansammlung/David Brandt 37 ab., l., ab.Mi., Staatskapelle Dresden/Matthias Creutziger 52 be., Staatliche Porzellanmanufaktur Meissen 57 ab., Villandry 44 be.